Hearts Bigger than Brazil

Just for you, Nancy:
"Beauty is truth, truth beauty,"—that is all ye know on earth, and all ye need to know.
Love,
Don

Hearts Bigger than Brazil

Poems by Don Perryman

Mountain Arbor Press

Copyright © 2021 by Don Perryman

All rights reserved. No part of this book may be reproduced or transmitted in any form or by any means, electronic or mechanical, including photocopying, recording, or any information storage and retrieval system, without permission in writing from the author.

ISBN: 978-1-6653-0245-6 - Paperback
eISBN: 978-1-6653-0246-3 - eBook

Library of Congress Control Number: 2021910873

This ISBN is the property of Mountain Arbor Press for the express purpose of sales and distribution of this title. The content of this book is the property of the copyright holder only. Mountain Arbor Press does not hold any ownership of the content of this book and is not liable in any way for the materials contained within. The views and opinions expressed in this book are the property of the Author/Copyright holder, and do not necessarily reflect those of Mountain Arbor Press.

Printed in the United States of America

⊚ This paper meets the requirements of ANSI/NISO Z39.48-1992 (Permanence of Paper)

Cover photograph: Santa Barbarinha Waterfall, Chapada dos Veadeiros, Cavalcante, Goias, Brazil.

In Memoriam

MISS MILDRED PERRYMAN
(1903 – 1989)

Of course this book is in your memory, you who brought me so many; read to me till I could read to you; taught me to make rhymes, explore woods, watch for snakes, play cards, curse like a sailor, sing parodies of church hymns, skip rocks over water, toast marshmallows, and catch fish. You passed along generations of priceless family lore and showed me how to love freely, fiercely – daring to be the man I'm still becoming.

Smoke and wind and fire are all things you can feel but can't touch. Memories and dreams are like that too. They're what this world is made up of. There's really only a very short time that we get hair and teeth and put on red cloth and have bones and skin and look out eyes. Not for long. Some folks longer than others.

If you're lucky, you'll get to be the one who tells the story: how the eyes have seen, how the hair has blown, the caress the skin has felt, how the bones have ached. What the human heart is like. How the devil called and we did not answer . . . . How we answered.

– *TOM SPANBAUER,* The Man Who Fell In Love with the Moon

Contents

Introduction . . . 1

Poetry is a search . . . 3

    Ars Poetica . . . 5
    Write! . . . 6
    How I've Written Poems . . . 8
    A Switch in Time . . . 10
    Noseeums . . . 11
    New Day . . . 12
    Any Port in a Storm . . . 13
    Why Not Walk & Whistle? . . . 15

Nature poets can't walk across the backyard . . . 19

    Worlds . . . 21
    Life on the Goldilocks Planet . . . 22
    Communion . . . 23
    Good Morning! . . . 24
    Fine Tuning . . . 25
    Vesper . . . 26
    Mutability . . . 27
    Seasoning . . . 28
    Fall Seduction . . . 29
    The Intensity of Bare Trees . . . 30
    Holiday Song . . . 31
    Late December . . . 32
    Rare Georgia Day . . . 33
    Ice Storm . . . 34
    Dawn at Bull Sluice Lake . . . 36
    Flowering . . . 37
    Heralds . . . 40
    April Again . . . 41
    Spring Festival . . . 42
    Mockingbirds . . . 43
    Cherry Trees Are Blooming Again . . . 45
    Tree . . . 46

The *Tao* . . . 47
Chattahoochee . . . 48
By the River . . . 51
Baptism . . . 53
Suwannee . . . 54
The Littoral Scene . . . 55
Loggerheads . . . 57
The Subgenual Prefrontal Cortex . . . 59
Eclipsed . . . 61
Plato's Cave . . . 62

I should not talk so much about myself . . . 63

Centering . . . 65
The Monkey Tree . . . 66
Lithia Springs, Georgia, 1949 . . . 67
Christmas Presence . . . 68
Sun Salutation . . . 70
Posture . . . 71
First Coming . . . 73
Formative Years . . . 74
Personas . . . 75
Suspension . . . 76
Customs of the Day . . . 77
Bi-polarity . . . 79
Good Intention . . . 80
Euphoriacs . . . 81
Full Disclosure . . . 83
Holding On & Letting Go . . . 85
What Ifs . . . 87
Best . . . 88
More Basic than Love . . . 89

Fate chooses our relatives . . . 91

Marcus . . . 93
Lena Shannon . . . 95
Crossing Palms . . . 96
Old Rhythms . . . 98
Salty Irreverence . . . 99
Familiarity . . . 102
The Widow . . . 106

Heart of Gold . . . 107
Weather Report . . . 108
Winter Aubade . . . 109
Trinity . . . 110
For My Niece, Graduating High School . . . 111
Home Scenes . . . 112
Fathers Wake . . . 113
Pretender . . . 114
Endgame . . . 115
The Treehouse . . . 116
Summer Inspiration . . . 117
Mildred's Garden . . . 118
Local Colors . . . 119
Just Don't Set Fire to the House! . . . 120
For Jessi & Michael on Your Wedding Day . . . 121

Friendship is born at the moment . . . 123

Thank You, Miss Edith . . . 125
Song for a Swan . . . 126
Friend . . . 127
Night Letter . . . 128
Letter Home . . . 129
Getting to Heaven . . . 130
Song for Solomon . . . 132
Haircuts . . . 133
Gardenias . . . 135
Plight . . . 136
Scrabble Buddies . . . 137
For the Woman at the Waffle House . . . 138

Love takes off the masks . . . 143

Maxims . . . 145
Song . . . 146
Afterglow . . . 147
Sundown on Cedar Key . . . 148
Unfound Lover . . . 149
How It Could Happen . . . 150
Romance . . . 155
Bedfellows . . . 156
The Broken Open Heart . . . 157
Old Roswell Cemetery . . . 158

Lightning . . . 160
Gift . . . 161
No Regrets . . . 162
Settlements . . . 163
Long-term Relationship . . . 165
Good Husbandry . . . 166
Departure . . . 169
They Call It Falling . . . 170
Don't Stop Kissing! . . . 172

Gladly would he learn . . . 175

Oral Book Reports . . . 177
Penmanship . . . 179
Formless Education . . . 181
Donors . . . 182
School . . . 183
Why I Hope You've Been Taking Notes . . . 184
Testing Instructions . . . 185
Goodbye, . . . 187
Was Melville Also Gay? . . . 188
For Marc . . . 191
Youth Counselor . . . 192
Therapeutic Observations . . . 194
Memento Mori . . . 196
Incident . . . 198
Vacation . . . 199
This Garden . . . 201
Observation . . . 204

One long cry from the heart of the artist . . . 205

Found Art . . . 207
Little Ode . . . 209
Across the Street & into the Hemingway House . . . 210
Door of the Heart . . . 213
Blockbuster Has Closed Its Doors . . . 215
Montage . . . 216
The Bigger They Are . . . 217
Bound to Be Read Books is Closing . . . 219
Instrumental . . . 221
Dark Time . . . 223

Travel is fatal to prejudice ... 225

> Vignette ... 227
> Cedar Key, 1955 ... 228
> *Viejo San Juan* ... 230
> San Juan Nocturne ... 231
> Still Night ... 232
> Star of Venus ... 234
> Last Liberty ... 235
> Crotalina ... 237
> Poem that Ends with the Word No ... 239
> The Bottlenose Dolphin ... 241
> Coastal Scene ... 243
> Cumberland Island ... 244
> Green Flash ... 245
> Gestures ... 247
> *Deux Mec* ... 249
> Flight of Fancy ... 251
> Morning Meals ... 252
> In the Shadow of the Moon ... 253
> Tunneling ... 258

There are more things in heaven ... 261

> Rude Awakening ... 263
> A Time & Place for Everything? ... 264
> Sources of Truth ... 265
> Plato's Sun ... 266
> Chuang Tzu & the Butterfly ... 268
> She Spoke Slowly, Seated like a Lotus ... 269
> Parable ... 270
> The Myth of Sisyphus ... 271
> Errand ... 273
> The Book of Truth ... 275

In my dreams the most charming forms ... 277

> Flying Dreams ... 279
> If You Must Take Notes ... 280
> What Do We Call Dreams like These? ... 281
> Sweet Dream ... 282
> Waking Dream ... 283
> The Dreamer ... 285

The Stillness . . . 287
Cut Off Head, Spite Face? . . . 289
Remembering Dreams . . . 291

Nothing is at last sacred . . . 293

Dress-up . . . 295
Faith . . . 296
Miracles & Gods . . . 297
Praise for Corn . . . 300
To Whom It May Concern . . . 302
Heavens . . . 303
Acts of God . . . 305
Wise Faith . . . 308

It's all a draft . . . 311

What Tiresias Knew . . . 313
Practice . . . 314
Bucket Lists . . . 318
Losses . . . 324
Old & New . . . 326
Ageing . . . 330
The Best Year of Your Life . . . 331
Seventy-five . . . 334
Apprehension . . . 335
Gratitude . . . 337
The End Is Near! . . . 338
Last Words . . . 340
Resolution . . . 341
Epitaph . . . 342
Promethean . . . 343
Not to Change the Subject, but . . . 344
Andy's Ride on the Merry-go-round . . . 345

Acknowledgements . . . 347

Introduction

Poetry – even the word can be off-putting if we had to sit through too many uninspiring English classes, and you may still find the subject as forbidding as I find calculus. Or maybe, like me, you do enjoy poems that offer appealing experiences and ideas without being riddles or puzzles. If you are, I hope these poems qualify.

As a poet and in other ways, I've always been an amateur, not a professional, except for those years when I was an English teacher – and even then money was never the real reward. I've always read and written poems for the sheer love of doing it, and for what I could learn from the effort. That's how I tried to teach them too.

Years ago at Westwood High School, the chemistry teacher told me he loved his job because, "When you think about it, everything is chemistry." "Yes," I quickly agreed – "or poetry," and we both laughed. I also recall what young Yuri Zhivago told his aunt when she asked him if he wanted to be a doctor or a poet. He told her that writing poems was not a profession; it was a sign of good health. I think he would have agreed that reading them is too.

Besides choosing from a lifetime of memories, thoughts, and dreams and wording them as best I could, I've posed questions and offered guesses here about things we aren't sure of – and how much do we know for sure anyway? We live in a marvelous, mysterious world, and these poems may just remind you of that.

This is not a short book, but for every poem here, dozens more that I've written over half a century failed to satisfy me enough that I was willing to share them. Out of the more than two hundred that *have* made the cut, only a fraction really delight me – and if you find some favorites too, then my first book will not be a failure.

I quote others a lot and sometimes use a line in more than one place if it really speaks to me. These noteworthy women and men have said some truly remarkable things, I think, and I count on their wit and wisdom to enhance my own efforts. I'd not be as far along as a poet or a person if so many of them hadn't blazed trails for me.

The quotations that begin each section introduce broad themes, but some poems could have fit just as well elsewhere. Where does a poem belong if it describes a dream about teaching? Poems about my family could easily be in the chapter on love. Some that I think of as philosophical also strike me as touching on the sacred.

I've known all along that however much I proofread and second-guess what I've written, I'll still find more things to change, even after I have the book in my hand. French poet Paul Valery wrote, "A poem is never finished, only abandoned." In light of that, I'm only half-joking when I say please rescue any that beg to be adopted.

Coleman Barks, a Southern poet I admire and recommend, ended one of his poems with this stanza which seemed to be very close to what I've been up to all along:

> *Fall flat before the altar of poemgiving*
> *and see if a friend is not tenderized*
> *into some fresh foolishness*
> *the two of you will never outlive.*

With that in mind, I hope you'll browse here at your leisure and find my foolishness entertaining. I'd be happy to hear what you think about any of it.

Don Perryman
Roswell, Georgia
May 2021

*Poetry is a search
for the inexplicable.*

– WALLACE STEVENS

Ars Poetica

As naturally as the oak bears an acorn, and the vine a gourd, one bears a poem.
– HENRY DAVID THOREAU

Gradually
can a poem be composed,

all required
a certain crafty patience,

humility for once
before a blank page,

audacity to labor forth
another metaphor –

yet ring by ring
a slender sapling grows.

1975

Write!

A line will take us hours maybe;
Yet if it does not seem a moment's thought,
Our stitching and unstitching has been naught.
Better go down upon your marrow-bones
And scrub a kitchen pavement, or break stones
Like an old pauper, in all kinds of weather;
For to articulate sweet sounds together
Is to work harder than all these, and yet
Be thought an idler. – WILLIAM BUTLER YEATS

As if I could
just up and decide,
Write a poem!
so that something good
would slip smoothly
from my consciousness
(whatever that may be)
via nimble fingertips
onto a keyboard,
across a monitor screen,
maybe even on to
an Internet post,
maybe spit out
from my trusty printer
onto a sheet of paper
I might share
with a few
indulgent friends.

It isn't enough
to wake up grateful
for more than I
usually even notice –
as I actually did
a few happy hours ago
from a long night's sleep
free of troubling dreams,
to gaze at one more gift
of blinding sunlight,

a roof reliably over us
through last night's rain,
generous hot mugs
of coffee for two –
a pristine Sunday,
hushed as a chapel
graced by kneeling nuns.

No, the whole thing
has to morph into words
worth sharing,
thoughts that reach
beyond the obvious,
the trite, the forgettable –
and I never think
for one complacent minute
I've surely done that,
however doggedly
I may have tried.

2016

How I've Written Poems

When ignorance is bliss, 'tis folly to be wise. – THOMAS GRAY

At first it seemed so easy:
I sprang my muse from a jail of rhyme and meter,
saw I could say most anything I damn-well pleased,
and then a whole cornucopia (a whole Pandora's box)
of red-hot images and ideas came blizzarding onto the page,
mixed metaphors and all.

I could pick anything, an ordinary day at the beach,
and let sounds and images wash up like driftwood.
White-hot sun knifed the whole scene without pity.
Bleached white shells dared stands of sea oats,
waving like gaunt prophets, to fling their colonies
of seed over a broad simplicity of sand
scrubbed by mumbling waves again, again.

Then all life's complications soon confused
and goaded me: this gigantic enigma,
a planet rife with all its joys and tragedies,
all in a cosmic chaos – dark, scintillating, vast!
not to mention a real doubt that anything really is
ticking on like the venerable old Newtonian clock
we clutch at like a corpse we can't abandon.

So I turned out complicated lines contrived
to grab that monstrous nightmare by its tail:
A groaning, heaving earth that labors round,
engendering its schizophrenic hordes –
not to mention my slipping grasp
at the even scarier images here within:
this brooding cavern of a brain that fires to render
ephemeral shadows of Plato's sunlit forms.

Chaos theory, Escher-sketch paradoxes,
fractals spawning endless ramifications
that just went right on multiplying freely

outside the frame of a monitor screen –
all of it began to sink in: Heisenberg's uncertainty,
Freud's id, Picasso's fractured caricatures –
not to mention Himmler's "Final Solution."
That cavalcade of flood, plague, war, and death,
and, well, just generally not knowing what's next
seemed to leave me precious little ground to stand.
And it wasn't just a movie or a nightmare anymore
(though I guessed even there I might be wrong).

But settling does come on with years,
an easy comfort within the whole unknowing,
quiet November evenings musing by a homely hearth
while shadows lengthen out of doors,
with me safe here inside, suspecting
all the old clichés, and their counterpoints, are true.

Dogged then, cheerful even, determined
to play out this dealt hand, incurable gambler
in a pirate cave of hearts, I bluff on right here
in the old game still, pretty sure it's rigged by pros
who even themselves are being scammed –
and me here, the consummate amateur!

You might catch me lounging now, for instance,
happily ignorant on a canopied riverbank
as shivers of glittering morning light on water
leap like minnows into the welcoming air.

I remind myself more often now, *Just breathe,
easily . . . gradually . . . freely . . .*
sighing within this soft, reliable breeze,
just as any other summer leaf that simply, greenly is –
oblivious to all its attendant ramifications,
and wasting not a second's thought of what to do next
as mercury falls – or rises.

198__

A Switch in Time

I'm laboring
this poem out by
all the latest guidelines, see:
street-corner imagery
focused to hawk-eye
sharpness, lines colloquial,
glib, candid as hell,
free at last of forced symbols
and literally ablaze
with high improbability,

when all at once
this massive Ferris wheel
flashing rainbows of neon
comes barreling down our street
toward me with who but
Ben Franklin himself
leaning out from the very
front seat, yelling
C'mon, man, get loose –
do your own thing.

1975

Noseeums

Cedar Key, Florida

Dots that zip right through
the mesh of window screen,
bite fiercer than mosquitoes,
scurry across the wooden table
even onto my typewriter page –

superfluous little punctuations!
I daub them up with an index finger,
roll them off, tiny black boogers,
into the wastepaper basket
and look for a final line to fill in here.

198_

New Day

On a clear day, you can see forever. – ALAN JAY LERNER

Let's just say that on this morning I spring up early,
easily from a side of the bed I'd never left before
to greet a shaft of sunlight beaming in at a blinding angle
through a grand window that opened up in the night
in a far wall of the bedroom that's now expanded
like a telescoping section in some fancy mobile home.

Instead of padding robed and slippered downstairs
to spoon regular grind into our compliant old coffeemaker,
customary sugar and creamer into slightly chipped mugs,
suppose I shock the boring routine of an ordinary day,
executing perfect Daffy-Duck back-flips, in my undies,
down a grand staircase, springy now as any trampoline.

Suppose too I find in the fridge an ornate goblet
of strange, sparkling elixir I don't recall buying,
then stride back up with it to sit at this familiar desktop –
but not to slog through the numbing news again
or compete with my on-line Scrabble opponents.
Instead, I blithely abandon all my tired routines –
and write this crazy poem instead.

2016

Any Port in a Storm

When things become so derivative as to become unintelligible, the same thing may be said for all of us, that we do not admire what we cannot understand.
– MARIANNE MOORE

In my own ongoing concern
for inspirational meanings,
ones that breathe
into my bone-and-skin-bound breast
a breeze from beyond,
I'm forever fondly seeking
a compass course of sorts,
one by which everything,
or at least a few plain things,
become clear enough
to further my voyage,
so to speak.

I have trouble though
with these surreal
stream of something-or-other
poems – like ones
that sometimes darken
pages of *The New Yorker*,
for example, however vogue
they've come to be these days.
They rarely offer channel buoys
or any lighthouse beacon,
any visible harbor
for my weathered wits.

Like weird dreams, such poems
evoke whatever they please
with little evident judgment
or least regard
for my determination
to get something, anything
out of their murk.

My best friend Richard
failed freshman lit,
a class where the professor
wanted him to see,
in a poem I never found,
Some rat represented God!
as he told me in disgust.
I wondered, discreetly,
how it might have.

I could be naive
to look for meanings
in any human work
that Nature herself hides.
Even a craggy waterfall
in all its flushing glory
simply says, *I fall* –
like Frost's taciturn star
that barely says, *I burn*.
Or maybe in truth
the water, the star
say nothing, nothing
nothing at all!

This turbulent
is-ness of existence
with no safe stanchion
anywhere to rope
my ship of thought
is an unsquared circle,
a mute Sphynx,
a Delphic Oracle,
priestess mouthing paradox.

It's the star that does not
even say, *I burn,*
although I surely do.

2012

Why Not Walk & Whistle?

How does a poem resemble a walk? — A. R. AMMONS

Why celebrate walking
and chewing gum
as if it were some clever
example of multi-tasking
that poor dolts can't accomplish?

Whistling, though!
Who remembers
who we first heard do it,
how we learned,
who our patient teacher
must have been,
or how difficult a task it was
until we finally got it,
that trick of the tongue?

But it's really a trick
of the human mind –
no, it's a gift from the heart –
that simple happiness
we sometimes feel
on any impromptu occasion,
whether we whistle or not.

Who taught us that?
Who instilled the carefree mood,
the marvelous inclination,
to suddenly, without forethought,
break into a cheerful tune –
not to mention just feeling
like humming along
in calm satisfaction,
in the sheer comfort
of an offhand moment?

Or did we learn to sing out loud
(the way you sometimes do),
and not as if no one's listening,
but as if the whole house
has suddenly paused to tune in.

That's how I heard
my mother singing more than once,
bent over another sink of dishes:

I love to tell the stoo-ry
of unseen thi-ings above!

As I know now
in my mid-seventies,
she was singing about heaven,
but with such a lilting voice
raised without restraint
that it seemed to me,
for all I could comprehend
at the innocent age of four,
that as she went about
her homely chores
the same as every other day,
she already was secure
in some sort of heaven,
(and heaven knows,
sometimes she wasn't,
though now I trust she is).

You too could be whistling
while you work,
or whistling for your supper,
or not just whistlin' Dixie,
but nervously whistling past
that proverbial graveyard,
lost in your own personal dark
under a hanging
scythe-like sliver of moon.

You could also be ambling along
as I happened to be this morning
over a bright van-Gogh palette
of crisp, fallen autumn leaves
in rare, peaceful solitude
graced with a glitter of sunlight,
when suddenly I was prompted
by such a liberated moment
to toss my gum, wet my whistle,
and offer up a carefree tune
that finally prompted this one.

2019

Nature poets can't walk across the backyard without tripping over an epiphany.

– CHRISTIAN WIMAN

Worlds

Other worlds exist, they say –
planets found, earth-like,
dozens of them now,
with decent atmospheres
and running water too,
without excess of ice or steam.

Those planets might be suited
well for complex life, we think,
in all its unpredictable
and multicolored incarnations,
such as we see here on ours.

Now multiply the dozens found
by the extension of a cosmos
beyond our sharpest scientific lenses
peering out and back with longest view,
toward some remote beginning
we're convinced it all once had.

There ought to be gazillions
more lives in gazillions more
locations besides just this one, right?

Or maybe not.
Suppose the odds of anything
like us are so astonishingly slight
we actually *are* alone,
however many almost-worlds,
almost alive, have circled other suns.

2011

Life on the Goldilocks Planet

We know this story well:
A mid-sized star nearby
(but not too near)
has made our habitation
not too frigid, not too stifling
for most of the lucky, happy time
and (till we juiced the heat)
just right for living here.

A fortunate rotation
makes our measured days
and nights conform conveniently
(hapless insomniacs excepted)
to our own circadian needs.

A tilt of axis alters seasons
such that flora bloom and ripen
(I'm only repeating an old refrain.)
till leaves, and later flakes perhaps, float down,
and the whole extravaganza
unfolds before our blasé eyes again.

Countless coincidings
I find to be so enigmatic,
so precise,* still come to be,
conspire to make us –
happy? free?
even awed and grateful
for such rich majesty?

2019

*The anthropic principle states that at the very beginning of time the physical variables in the universe had to be precisely set to make possible our galaxies, stars, and planets – on at least one of which humans like us could evolve to marvel at how it all began, billions of years ago

Communion

This massive, reeling ball
of brown-green rolling hills
and blue-green roiling ocean
has some great geographic

syntax all its very own.
We only think it calls on us
to make its meaning known.
But we are isolate, contrary,

lacking the atonement
of rocking wave, rooted grove.
We live de-natured, one remove
from massive green reality.

So in our conscious need
we delve to understand,
explore this treasured land,
plunge in its circling sea.

1972

Nature poets can't walk across the backyard . . .

Good Morning!

October 19, 2016

This sphere we ride
has once again
turned itself
as it always does
toward dawning sun,
our source of all
that energizes,
coaxes leaflets
out of the earth
to make a spring,
then by autumn slant
gently urges leaves
to turn and fall,

yet on this morning
warms our skins and lights
our woodland way
to a favorite waterfall.
Where else in jet-
black, star-stud void
might such precision
possibly hold sway?
Today I speculate
that possibly here
in our lucky world alone
does all creation coincide
so flawlessly to make
just such a day.

Fine Tuning

Now at last they've picked up
the great, intergalactic *Om*,
echo of a billion-years-ago beginning.
And right back down here
on air-conditioned earth,
we observe the covert complaints
of a laboring human heart
beeping its green luminescence
across an oscilloscope screen.

Yes,

but what are we tuning out,
what's the great, proverbial
price we pay with no consideration?
Ask the unreadable stones
in this overgrown graveyard,
ask the mute bones beneath them.
They can tell you something too,
but you have to listen close,
and you have to want to know.

198_

Vesper

Tonight I glimpsed a beacon
moon beaming full in summer haze,
rolling steadily toward us
like some massive pearl,
or even cream-faced Venus,
rising above the tide reliably.

Some moments are so fine,
so exquisitely situated in time,
we live our lives to have them,
though we may be desperate
for days empty as the space
between us and that cratered orb.

See the ancient sign her features make:
silver teardrop swirling up one way,
grey paisley curling down the other –
to represent the light and dark
of things? To make us guess
where Asian sages got that sign?

In spite of all determined science,
beyond the mysteries of creeds,
thrives simply this, this way
the mind and senses work and play.
I stopped my writing here,
took binoculars back outside,

perched myself atop the porch rail,
propped a pillow over the eave,
and settled up there well, to spy
through an amplitude of sky
on that luminary sphere,
its mountains and its mares
pulsing to my heartbeat in the lenses.

1984

Mutability

I glance idly down
at the sun-struck asphalt
and imagine I see the shadow
of a fluttering butterfly.

Looking up to verify
I realize my would-be
living creature is instead
a dead but twirling maple leaf,

which got me to anticipating
the coming chill of autumn
to end another endless summer,
although it *is* still August.

I should be happy now
with that transfigured image
offering its hint of mutability
mourned by those Romantic poets.

2018

Seasoning

How many summer sunsets
do green trees require
to fill their living leaves
with ruddy fire?

I don't presume to know,

but I am neither first
nor last to see and say
that nature riots most
near end of day.

197_

Fall Seduction

The maple on the street
frees itself of curling
crimson-saffron leaves
from upmost limbs on down.

I see a Gaugin girl
let fall her flowery array
to raise up eager arms
and hold a golden lover.

1972

The Intensity of Bare Trees

Naked trunks and limbs thrust up from earth
to hands with fluttering fingers spread to sky.
Deeply rooted and steady they stand,
appealing to gods gone far and cold.

Their poignant patience thrills me
here facing the fall and winter dark.
I want just such a natural intensity,
such poise against the inevitable.

I want this poem as well to appeal,
enliven any leafless constitution,
remind the sullen sap to bide its time,
await with confidence a distant spring.

1990

Holiday Song

In the midst of winter, I finally learned there was in me an invincible summer.
– ALBERT CAMUS

At the turn of the year,
in our darkest, cold season
when stars beam their brightest
for some winter reason,

we gather round tables
to feast by our fires.
We tell homely stories.
and know something higher

that comes at this crux
of the year to inspire us,
something that shelters
and clearly requires us.

Call it the spirit
or angels or such,
or call it that Buddha
in each of us.

But it's surely what sages
would have us esteem:
Call it the Mystery
(with capital M).

Or think of our elders
(in spirit or shape)
walking here with us,
each move we make.

Oh, call it Jehovah,
Goddess or Zeus,
but know it as that which
we never will lose.

And just as our star-sun
rises each year
toward new spring warmth,
we turn from our fears,

we settle our sorrows,
our angers, our blame
(and all those wee demons
that put us to shame).

And we celebrate wholeness.
We pause to be still,
to know the All-loving.
We trust that we will.

199_

Late December

Snow is flaking fast
onto black-leafed walks,
frost-crazed windshields,
iced boxwoods and lawns.

It shakes its clean sheets out,
to shroud a dead landscape –
dry sage, abandoned bike,
stripped curbside Yule tree.

This snow will surely last
long enough at least
to rest an outworn year
silently, discreetly.

1972

Rare Georgia Day

Somewhere up there hosts of angels must be shaking
a year's worth of heavenly cloud-dust from their hair.
Or maybe they're shearing celestial flocks of sheep.
Perhaps it's a sky of confetti with all natural ingredients.
Or else, they might be masses of tiny white aliens invading.

More likely, ordinary raindrops are simply bursting
like popcorn way up in the freezing stratosphere.
And how *do* those countless flakes avoid each other?
Are they charged to stay apart the whole way down?
Could they be colliding, clumping, flocking earthward?

If so, might they start high enough and fall long enough
to become snowballs – or snowfolk! – before crash-landing?
It's a relief that instead only little kiss-sized, white bouquets
are now fluttering shamelessly onto our lips and down
our sleeves while we stand in the open doorway amazed.

So now we get to stay at home, enjoy a Snow Day.
If need be, we'll crunch an icy trek to the grocery store.
We can visit our neighbors, celebrate a bonus holiday,
build fires, sip cocoa, make love, take naps, read books –
or just play music and vegetate here with the house plants.

We might even discover how a rare surprise like this,
totally out of the ordinary, but not too unsettling,
can shake us again from our clock-and-calendar routines
so that the Mystery we blithely call the life we know
wakes us up again from everything we ever supposed.

1995

Ice Storm

If winter comes . . . − PERCY BYSSHE SHELLEY

Sleety snow is hissing, freezing
into perilous contortions
like too much cold,
hard truth at once.

An evidently massive
black tree limb down the street
gives up its ghost and pitches
down in darkness.

From its crashing chandelier,
shards skitter across concrete,
shattering the eerie quiet
of a dormant winter night.

Mid-morning, I might dare
to navigate the grey-white
minefield out of doors
to get what mail has made it here

or just to stretch cramped limbs,
fog the sullen air with breath,
tamp down by venturing out
my creeping cabin fever.

Lumbering earth
will ease back coyly
into its annual on-again,
off-again courtship

with our nearest star
for one more fling next spring,
just as it always has,
releasing this god-awful freeze,

softening the ground again
to thrust up green
spears, buds from bulbs
into celebratory blooms

year after year after year –
like the countless times
I eulogize their charms.
But that's merely a theory

this frigid winter night
as another leafless limb
of a nervous window tree
comes tapping at our peace.

We turn to ease ourselves
along each other, grateful
for the gift of winter sleep,
and for our banked heat.

2015

Dawn at Bull Sluice Lake

eyes too busy to know a blessing – FRANKLIN ABBOTT

I park my car so winter-early yet,
the dark dome of heaven's still star-glittered,
even as it pales in the east to blues and grays.

Racks of mackerel cloud roll out
plowed furrows of condensation,
like waves in a slo-mo surf.

Now off below the horizon, unseen sun
blushes the under-belly of each one,
silhouetting that distant line of trees.

I feel restless, almost guilty
when I slip into these epiphanies,
as if I were sneaking into Someone's garden.

I was about to drive away, miss this crescendo,
tangerine in my lap half-eaten, ego-thoughts rushing me.
Here the dawn comes now – what a glittering extravaganza.

1992

Flowering

Never to allow gradually the traffic to smother with noise and fog the flowering of the spirit. – STEPHEN SPENDER

Always I marveled
how a squiggly groove
in a black vinyl disc
could channel so well
young Judy Garland's innocence
wafting *Over the Rainbow*.
Or how it is that mute piano keys
ever unlock Chopin,

how a swiftly scanning beam
inside that old cathode tube
gave us not just Popeye cartoons
or even the best of *Father Knows Best*,
but some memorable thing
transcending all the silly sit-coms
laced with cunning commercials –
like the night *All in the Family*
rose eloquently out of its weekly self
to articulate, beyond mere liberal theme
or even laugh-out-loud humor,
something undeniable and worthy
about our common condition,
our uncommon promise,
leaving viewers here in our darkened
living room, eyes glistening
while the luminescent credits
glide musically up the screen.

So many proofs of efflorescence:
how out of a frigid week in February
sprouts a day of blossoms you could swear
belong in the sunny heart of April,

how in ten or fifteen billion years,
they say, the universe swirled
up this blue-green world,

how leathery old cactuses
manifest pastel, tissue-thin blooms
among the countless thorns
to beautify the dry desert air,

how the merest infant smiles
for the first time up into your face,
becoming the Christ-child, the Buddha
for just that marvelous pause,

how any unpremeditated instant
may take us entirely out of time
and all our mundane troubles
to offer a love, a joy that sustains us.

The evidence is astounding:
how Thoreau, transcendental eccentric
scribbling in his hut by the pond or hoeing his beans,
cultivated rapport with the likes of Gandhi and King,

how crazed, inspired van Gogh
swirled up bouquets of sunflowers,

how that old meddler, Polonius,
belabored the young Laertes
with a parental catalog of dos and don'ts
and then outspoke himself
with such ironic eloquence:
This above all, to thine own self be true.

It might even happen when you hear
the unlikeliest dullard in your own life
say something so apt –
a least favorite uncle maybe,
drunk and voluble at some boring family event –

confide, hand cupped to your ear,
with a clarity and confidence
you never heard from him before,
enunciating each word slowly
without slurring a one:

*When we're willing
and lucky, dear fellow,
just being here alive
in a world so amazing
is far and away
too marvelous to explain.*

*We work
and we wait
to watch it all flourish.*

199_

Heralds

Yesterday out back
I kidnapped three oblivious, early-bird
daffodil blooms.

(I've apologized before and will again,
for doting on them every year.
They were Mildred's favorite too.)

I imagined, perhaps naively,
I was saving them
from the frost forecast last night.

I brought them in,
filled a wine bottle with water,
threaded the stems down its neck,
and left them there at the sink.

This morning I pad down
bath-robed, slippered, still half-
wandering in a winter dream,
to make our wake-up coffee.

I'm leaning in to the faucet
(where they're standing
overlooked)
to fill the pot as usual.

But what an unforeseen aroma
that words can never conjure
(except maybe to say, *Remember?*)
startled me with its redolence
sent out from yellow trumpets –

spring!

2014

April Again

Released from winter's inarticulate freeze,
escaped from barren months of indoor pacing
in forced hot air when no words graced a page,
he slips outdoors in shirtsleeves, lets fresh breeze
tickle his skin, lets sun warm cold, pale limbs.

He's early up and out, free of a workday week,
as others doze through this old surprise of spring.
The backyard weeping willow's in tiny, lime-green leaf,
a light-winged congregation's flitting, fluting
pertly up and down its slim, cascading limbs.

Given countless seasons of such imagery,
his own reporting sounds superfluous.
Each year the little lines, however crafty,
carry in their echoes more presumption.
Why not re-read Chaucer? Housman? Frost?

Yet every April brings out something new.
Woods, roadside fields, green garden beds,
even a neglected ditch along the freeway,
all have wherewithal to renovate their variegation.
Just so, the sap of this stalled pen can flow again.

197_

Nature poets can't walk across the backyard . . .

Spring Festival

The flowering peaches in back
have bulging grey waists
hollowed a bit by years,
but the gnarled old pair
still know how to ease pale
leaflets, poke forth new tips,
make minute buds again
that open out to fireworks
of pink pom-pom blooms –

only to cut them loose,
blowing a breezy diaspora
that pastels flowerbeds,
glues pop-art to wet walkways,
quilts our car windshields,
and polka-dots the patio.

We track crushed bits
of blossom-petal confetti
even into the house with us,
littering the afterglow
of this annual fiesta.

2017

Mockingbirds

For days now
those two have harried
Catherine the Great Cat
from crepe myrtle and sycamore
out in my front yard.

You can see bent-down patches
in the monkey grass
where she's lurked, immobile,
under siege – the whole time
stalking them in turn, ineffectively,
yearning for a throb of bird flesh
through feathers skewed by claws,
instinctively rehearsing
her toothsome *coup de grace.*

I think I know just how she feels.
I barge right out to get the mail,
to leave the trash can at the curb,
or just to shoo them briefly away,
tired of their endless *chip, chip, chee.*

I so much bigger than either of them, or Kate,
remain powerless to stop their constant noise.
I think she thinks I ought to be her champion,
or else she thinks that blundering human
comes only to complicate her tireless wait.

Yesterday I went out and shot them
with a quick stream from the garden hose,
scaring them off across the street,
scaring Kate in through her cat door too.

Shortly afterward,
a neighbor from over there
knocked on my door to tell me
those two birds have also been driving

Nature poets can't walk across the backyard . . .

her poor old calico up the blinds all week,
adding that she saw their chick
flopping about the yard two days ago.

We speculate: dead, perhaps, already?
Was all that bird-noise lamentation,
condemnation of all killers?

As I write this now, I notice,
for the first time, a creepy silence.
I go down to check and find them gone.

Inside, Kate's splayed
on the living room floor
licking her silky haunches.

1995

Cherry Trees Are Blooming Again

Loveliest of trees, the cherry now
Is hung with bloom along the bough,
And stands about the woodland ride
Wearing white for Eastertide. – A. E. HOUSMAN

We see you got the word again:
Our planet's heating up. We're partly to blame
(entirely to blame for the withering heat of our wars).
We hardly deserve another efflorescence
as breathtaking, inexplicable as you.

But here you are everywhere anyway:
gracing roadsides, fields, cemeteries, yard on yard,
lifting nonchalant limbs skyward again,
tossing creamy ecstasies to the breeze
just beyond our busy, downcast eyes.

Little you care it's still March, not April,
this year even hotter than others,
or that ironic winter ice threatened your limbs.
Little you care you're blithely ignored,
all but shrouded in exhausting human clouds.

What a shame to marginalize you, though.
In passing we should offer more than a glance,
or maybe even quit our silly errands
to rest ourselves at your grassy feet
in wordless awe and devotion.

For you sentinels are far wiser than we,
assuming a lot less than we claim to know,
you innocent omens of oncoming heat.
But you have no need to forgive us, perfect trees,
gifts with no use for our guilt – or our gratitude.

2007

Tree

In a spacious, furrowed field
by a straight-line highway,
or on a bare hilltop –
even on a remote islet
you might be boating past,
you'll see one:

a freely flourishing tree
uncrowded, unencumbered,
with nothing to the horizon
to shade her spread,
except at end of day
the turning earth itself.

Rooted and established,
she stands on fertile ground
trunk, limbs, leaves
burgeoning up and out,
gargantuan broccoli crowns
in vibrant green display.

Imagine this scene:
a fine old live oak, say,
nothing else for acres,
luxuriating mid soil and sky
heavy low limbs boughing
onto solid ground.

What a wholesome
head of olive-green
with a silent *Here I am*
to anyone who might
be apt enough to see
perfection.

2017

The *Tao*

The static oscillation
of wobbling leaves
is a trembling of trees
bending upward into
a swirling yin-yang
of cloud tatters swirling
leisurely leeward.

Think of a feathery
van Gogh, unweighted
by any hint of madness,
thoroughly impregnated
one hue with another
till the whole scene's one
shimmering inspiration.

197_

Chattahoochee

1.

Start at dawn on a Saturday
as horizontal sun filters through
black silhouettes of buildings and trees
to enforce its glitter and warmth
over the grey haze of Georgia.

Go Roswell Road to Morgan Falls Road
that winds past fields and a huge land-fill
where orange dirt is bulldozed smoothly
over everybody's junk and garbage.

Hike down to a broad sweep of river
where an ageing hydroelectric dam
holds back a silty lake upstream
and doles it down in sheets
where men in boats are casting lines
near concrete portals posted
Danger Stay Clear.

Take the path downstream
past folk and their kids fishing
with bamboo poles and old-world patience.
Follow a sinuous route
that's worn the hillside riverbank
over, around, and even under boulders
through laurel and rhododendron
half a mile to where pines twist from crevices
to stand imperially along stony cliffs
that rise above a grey-green spread of river.

2.

See where climbers come
with their girlfriends and coolers of beer
to work their way up the rock face,

lusty lovers, attempting precarious holds,
grasping curves and juts and clefts of stone,
then fastening ropes to tree trunks at the top
and rappelling themselves off the edge, bounding
backward down to the flat clay bank.

Watch now one blond young champion
run on his rope to leap face-forward off the edge
and down his zinging trajectory,
not touching rock or slowing descent with his grip
till just before he lands splat on his confident feet,
and the entire cliffside echoes
in whistles and cheers and applause.

3.

Go a little farther now
till you find yourself a solitary ledge
where the biggest ruddy-barked pine of all
soars up from a cliffy conglomerate of ancient rock
where you think of the age-old hymn
that means more here and now than it ever did
on Baptist Sundays of your childhood.

Here in the natural stillness,
you command a bird's-eye view:
aquamarines of shimmering Chattahoochee,
with visible streaks of bottom
silt and sand and river stone
in the wide, wide course of things.

Westward, across the river, broom sage fields
give way to hills of pine and hardwood.
And, excepting the inevitable
jar or can or cigarette butt,
you could be here in another time entirely
cooled by updraft currents, redolent
of mossy banks and soil and river life.

A muskrat forages along the far shore,
its wake a tell-tale vee.

Comfortable, immobile on your ledge,
cross-legged if you please,
spine upright, arms at rest,
hands over knees,
breathing easily now,
think about nothing at all
but the sheer ambiance of the instant,
its subtle rustlings, twitterings,
shimmerings in sunlight.

And if you're lucky at all,
as the crisp atmosphere breezes
freely in and out of you,
you'll know a spot of time
the old Muscogee surely knew
when they sat the self-same way
taking in this grand, oblivious scene.

198_

By the River

Swirls of current
nibble away at shoreline,
moving crumbles of silt,
brown clutches of leaves
in and out of the flow.

The broad stretch of grey-green water
threads around stones into pools
where ducks and geese paddle and bob.

And the lackadaisical clouds
ride high winds spinning
paisley wisps of white and gray.

And the leaning ranks of trees
poke out minute springtime buds
that swell to air and light.

And the path along the river
threads among these turnings, urgings.

And this breathing, this heartbeat
keeps inscrutable time
with a mind-blowing flow.

Ambling amid all the sights
and sounds and smells of things,
remember a winter walk
on crunching needles of ice,
anticipate another summer swim.

And in such way
time past and future slip their presence
into the great vernal flow
of bird flutings and trillings,
sway of glad green trembling treetops,
an everywhere of filtered sunlight,

Nature poets can't walk across the backyard . . .

and the proverbial ten thousand things,
all suffused in lightest breeze.

This heaving, subtle flux:
in a single breath a blossom eases open,
shadows of leaf-dance, limb-dance
wobble across a sandy path.
Green water glugs and gutters
among stones round and plump as loaves,
freshness of drenched moss-banks,
all the invisible perching and crawling,
urgent callings, evasions of life
teeming in earth, air, water, and sun.

This fecund instant, shine and shade,
omnipresent array of manifest existence
is encompassed by the mind, grasped and held,
to make a lasting vision, make it whole.

1987

Baptism

Shed
clothes
and sprint
down a
slope to a
waiting shore
where limpid
water
welcomes
slender
limbs.

Plunge
deep,
skimming
the weed
along the
bottom,
freeing
trails of
bubbles
tickling
up the sides
of fish-white
thighs.

Surface
sleekly,
forehead
moonward,
treading
endless
ripples
round
a torso's
buoyant
motion.

Stroke
to shore,
stand
and squeeze
lake mud
and more
bubbles up
through toes.

Shiver
into a
late spring
stillness.
Grant the self
this dripping,
shivering
earth
return,
this birth.

198_

Suwannee

Even the weariest river winds somewhere safe to sea.
– ALGERNON CHARLES SWINBURNE

Suwannee starts out swampy,
more of an ooze than a flow,
drains down out of Georgia
syrupy like Coca Cola
between flat fields of Florida,
beneath palmettos, skeleton trees,
crows, over dark tea leaves of silt,

white sands of seas long gone,
stands of cypress knees,
gnarled trunks and limbs
of greybeard live oaks
leaning over her shoulders –
she as sleek and innocent
as Susanna among the elders.

Suwannee's dark and slow.
She pools and swirls her
spreading tresses lazily
along, until, as if by indiscretion,
unfurls sinuous dark curls
into the reach of the great,
green Gulf of Mexico.

198_

The Littoral Scene

Underneath our feet
salt-white sand
weathers down
and heaps up here
by ghostly driftwood limbs,

a trove of vacant shells,
pink claw, grey feather,
bleached-out bit of bone.

Splayed before our gaze
horizontal bands
of grey, green sea
shimmer like a fresh van Gogh,
weighted by that same
escape from madness,
each glittery brush stroke
wildly twirled
mid tide and breeze.

All up and down the shoreline
roiling surf slops its paisleys
onto a swath of sand,
over, over, over again.

Shoreward, hardy stands of sea oats
sway fronds like wheat,
like fingers of prophets
along wind-wafted dunes,
sawing in unison as if to point us
upward
toward some celestial omen.

But all we see is lofty
cotton-clumps of cloud
rolling along the horizon
in endless illusions of stillness.

Nature poets can't walk across the backyard . . .

Higher yet,
an amplitude of azure,
distantly feathered in spotless gulls,
all struck in chrome-white
radiance of sun.

We think this scene has meaning.
It needs none.

198_

Loggerheads

Bright fall Cumberland morning,
we start our leisurely backpack
five modest miles for *homo sapiens*
on a sandy path to our campsite up the island.

We sidetrack to the beach and spot a crew
of natural resource workers
releasing a score of turtle hatchlings,
nest washed out by a recent storm,
freed here from their rescue incubation.

Olive drab, hardly over an inch,
some trail their empty yolk sacs.
All inscribe flipper tracks in sand.

(We're told to keep our shadows off
of their determined motion.)

They're making bee-lines toward the sun
hanging obliquely to the shoreline
above the wide and deep Atlantic.

Suppose they'd been let go
one afternoon, sun luring them
over a whole impassible continent.

Not all of them aim well now, either.
A couple haven't budged.
One spirals back toward the dunes
as if to retreat to its nest again
till redirected by a hand.

Odds are weighty against a one
lasting in that vast food chain,
even if guidance is better than good.

They make intricate parallel tracks
anyway, down the wet shoreline,
undaunted tiny daubs, leaving Chinese
characters that quote *I Ching**:
Perseverance furthers.

1996

*The I Ching *or* Book of Changes, *known as the oldest text still in existence, is an oracle based on yin and yang, represented by solid or broken lines that, according to legend, were first seen and deciphered by the Chinese ruler Fu Hsi in the third millennium B. C. – from patterns on the back of a tortoise shell. "Perseverance" is a word that appears frequently in the book.*

The Subgenual Prefrontal Cortex

One impulse from a vernal wood
May teach you more of man,
Of moral evil and of good,
Than all the sages can. – WILLIAM WORDSWORTH

It's a mouthful
I just learned to say,
a bit of the brain
that activates
when we brood,
as we commonly do,
obsessing irritably about
the car with a worrisome knock,
how the sinus surgery will go,
an odd-shaped spot
on the back of a hand,
how I raised my kids,
a frown on the face of a spouse –

not to mention
radical extremes
in the Near East
(or here at home),
Fukushima's toxic spew,
whether the next election
will take us onward or back,
why the credulous still kowtow
to egomaniacal demagogues
who dog our lives –
what the finale will be.

The article said that nature,
even a stroll in a park,
deactivates that part,
that nagging little scold
with the ponderous name
that thinks it knows
we need to worry.

Tonight though,
you and I lounge amicably
out back on the patio
where no mosquito bite
begins to raise an itch,
where glaring day is dimmed
and no siren screams.

And just then
up through twilit haze,
I glance and chance to see
in stillest silvered sky
a milky little half full moon.

And in this bright scintilla
of onward-flowing time,
a tiny silhouette of bird
swoops in twixt sky
and my arched eyes,
inscrutable black mote
merged instantly
into the black welcome
of those woods,

my subgenual prefrontal cortex
and yours as well, I trust,
significantly eased.

2015

Eclipsed

January 20, 2019

Total lunar eclipse and rare super blood wolf moon bedazzle star-gazers.
– CNN

That was last night.
By the time I thought of it
and ran out in the black cold,

it was a full, white pearl up there,
one-third bitten into
by our own shadow.

I called Gilson out, shivering,
got him to utter his understated *Wow*
before we retreated to artificial heat and light.

I reminded myself
to make sure to check later
to be right out there when

we'd covered it up completely
making our pale satellite
look just like red planet Mars,
only up close now.

But I forgot,
went back to absorbing some TV show.
Maybe we'll be around for the next one.

Plato's Cave

We cannot comprehend
this universe, but think a cage
of golden wires wherein we find
another ancient live oak
in whose arching limbs a house-
boat labors the turbulent swells
in a steaming pot of herbal tea
served in a formal garden
long disregarded – yet still
glimpsed in a fading sketch
drawn by an idle Zen novitiate
who then takes one of many
paths from Plato's cave.

Extending this admittedly
simplistic metaphor,
we can hint at the bafflement
of scientific minds today
who are now asking, in effect,

*How on earth does such a cage
come to be in such a cave?*

198_

I should not talk so much about myself if there were anyone else I knew as well.

– HENRY DAVID THOREAU

Centering

The universe is an infinite sphere, the center of which is everywhere, the circumference nowhere. – BLAISE PASCAL

There is no preferred frame of reference. – ALBERT EINSTEIN

Before the heliocentric bright idea dawned,
astronomers and divines burned midnight oil
arranging motions of all the heavenly bodies
to make our minute planet, like their God, unmoving.

Such a point of view forced byzantine loop-the-loops
on all the other spheres – increasingly entangled
the farther out those guessers managed to gaze.
But not only earth can be assumed the center.

We can all-too-easily imagine everyone else
and every other object in the wide universe
dancing in dedicated arabesques – around ourselves!

Although I've sensed it just that way before
and probably will indulge myself so fondly again,
conceit won't prove that point of view, or win a friend.

2018

The Monkey Tree

Twilight and bedtime now
for a play-worn four-year-old
alone in a big maple bed.

Still at last, head cupped in a pillow,
he gazes dimly out at a round
black-leafy silhouette of tree – *ah!*
the one he wanted to climb today.
Sun subsides behind it now
in scattering veins of gold.

Suddenly, all that dark
mandala animates
before his sleepy eyes.

Oh, it's little monkeys!
he almost says out loud.

Shadowy and magical,
they clamber, swing, cavort
all up and down, around
their jungle gym of limbs.

Long, long, he fascinates,
quasi-superstitious little kid
caught now between his waking
and the rest that's on its way.

He eyes them now, hypnotic,
counts chimps, gymnastic dozens,
until, almost as slowly
as ebb of guileless day,
his innocent (if hardly ignorant)
eyes close.

2004

Lithia Springs, Georgia, 1949

The futuristic Southern Crescent
blares into startled, small-town evening,
churning streamlined green/white diesels
trailing silver cars of windowed strangers.

A bright room of well-dressed diners
zooms nonchalantly on to foreign lands.

She skirrs along wheel-polished rails;
shakes gravel-bedded, creosote ties;
then vanishes into a red-banked curve
to horn her way through more towns on her line,

setting other child-hearts pounding.

197_

I should not talk so much about myself . . .

Christmas Presence

Notice how
if something unforgettable
happened when you were young,
you might slip into a habit
of telling listeners things like this:

*When I was a kid
we always used to go out
on a cold November morning
and find the perfect spruce
to cut from our woods.*

*We'd haul it home to decorate
through the afternoon,
and then we'd sit around
drinking hot chocolate,
savoring the magic of the season.*

*Dad would flip a switch,
and the room would go dark
except for the tree lights
and their reflections on
all the glittering baubles,
and oh man, that's how
Christmas ought to be.*

Well, for your information
all of that did happen,
all the time
when I was a kid.

At least every Christmas.
Well, four or five of them.
Or maybe even fewer.

And I guess the tree
was only an ordinary

Georgia slash pine
from our neighbor's woods,
with their permission,
because actually we had
just the dilapidated old place
on the one hardscrabble acre
there by the railroad track.

And we never had hot chocolate either.
That and the spruce
came decades later.

So I embellished a bit.

But the winter night
and the lights?
I remember them.

And a dazzling white star
atop that tree –
that star I'm sure of most of all,
even when I can't recall
the presents.

198_

Sun Salutation

I have thoughts that are fed by the sun. – WILLIAM WORDSWORTH

Atop the family acre
the old grey garage
of corrugated zinc on steel
waxed warm in dawn-light
while most of the homeplace
remained in shadow.

I sought that sun-kissed
leeward side, stood gingerly
behind a row of orange daylilies
for oblivious minutes
before my half-mile walk
to another school adventure.

I pressed, eyes closed,
against the radiant
alloy, hot to my palms,
took in morning energy
radiating my own
as if I were also a sun.

2019

Posture

Everyone strikes a pose.
Mother admonished me,

Stand up straight,
hold your shoulders back.

I heard her saying, *Be a man.*
But I was a curved kid,
a skinny one, other boys would say,
bent over submissively
shielding my belly from a gut-punch
I kept expecting to come
from one of the redneck bullies
in that provincial town.

She also admonished me,

You're just like your daddy.
You don't know how to relax.

It was hard, given the pre-teen vow
I took when he died
never to need anyone so badly
and lose again that way.

I was relaxed at times, though,
inclined forward in that fifth-grade classroom
when Katherine Hood had us sing,

O'er the lake we gaily go,
hol-de-re-dee-ya, hol-de-yah!

Some guessed I sang that song too gladly,
but that happy boatman's chant seems lost,
nor do we have songs of the Senoi and the Hopi
who didn't always hold their shoulders back either,
though we can still see them, inscrutable and tall,

I should not talk so much about myself...

proud, present, breasting the world
like the prows of long ships parting waves.
ready to face the heavens with prayers,
engage for good or ill with their neighbors,
change falling dreams to flying,
even as they slept.

So I inhale, horse stance,
as taught in T'ai Chi classes,
shoulders down and back, chest open,
giving the heart its room to throb,
the lungs their space to fill and empty,
relaxed and fancy free.

Arms sweep a circle up on high
palms up until they meet overhead
then curve down past me,
knees slightly bending,
a breathing benediction
with exhalation, bringing the hands,
palms down, gently to usher out
any remaining stress and air.

Up and over and in again,
down to another *namaste*,
further down to my sides
then round again,
till body and spirit hum
in spherical harmony.

Dull throb of sturdy heart.

Flow with the *Tao*,
be a conduit. Be here now.
Shoulders back . . . down . . . relaxed.
Breathe.
Be all my mother wished for me.

2015

First Coming

My Victorian childhood
home is now
the Sunday School building
of the Full Gospel Tabernacle
on Temple Street
in Lithia Springs, Georgia,
a town that slipped
from mineral spa to shabby suburb
in a few predictable decades.
The wrap-around veranda,
once my rampart
against the redneck neighborhood,
is dressed up now
in windowless white clapboards –
a wistful pregnancy planned
to quicken the Christ-child again.

In my wildest delusion
I return some day,
a teacher, a prophet even,
opening blind eyes,
healing the faithful.
And the gathered throng
will move unanimously
to sanctify the lofty
magnolia treetop where,
swaying amid glossy oval leaves
and creamy blossoms
and all that pungent, natural urging,
I once clenched its tapered spire
and shocked myself
into my own first coming,
gaping off through spring haze
at the still impossibly distant
twin mounts of Kennesaw.

1975

Formative Years

Was it cold that formed me, bedrooms
unheated, old putty-crazed windows,
water shut off in the ground
on sub-freezing nights –

or maybe sheet blankets,
kerosene-soaked kindling, coal
fed into a Franklin stove
in our humble living room?
Oatmeal remembered
as neither tasty nor bad?

Or was it red applesauce
scooped out from mason jars
in sweet, hearty chunks
onto buttered white-bread toast
stroking the palate, stoking
the sensitive gut of a skinny-shy boy,
headaches and nausea never explained?

Was the county school an asylum,
or pine woods inviting adventure,
neighbor boys offering fun and fear,
needles piercing, but measles
and mumps running their courses
in boring, sunlit sick-beds
redeemed by escapades in pages of books?

Rock-shattered windows at Halloween,
amiable mutt long since abandoned?

Ancestral home (razed and replaced now):
cold or the warmth that defied it,
trouble or love that made me
the human I am?

2019

Personas

I am not Prince Hamlet, nor was meant to be. – T. S. ELIOT

I confess,
I identified with the fiddling grasshopper,
not the season-wise ants who showed him mercy
when the weather turned bad.

I felt more like Rabbit who hopped way ahead,
then lay back on a lush green bed of over-confidence
nibbling like Bugs Bunny at a carrot end
while elder, wiser Tortoise lumbered along to the finish,
carrying that quaint reptilian humility of his.

Donald was my favorite namesake
striding out with his trio of duckling nephews in tow,
then convulsing and quacking in ruffled exasperation.

I was Charlie Brown, playing well with others,
but tricked into bungling the kickoff,
screaming *Aaaarrrggghhhh!* with cartoon hands
spread wide to the heartless heavens.

Cautiously I eyed those dashing super-heroes
comically arrayed in muscular tights, on the scene
at once, working marvelous good in the world.
But I was not like them, no, not me.

Maybe I'm Frederick, that wee storybook mouse
who lounges about as his fellows store up grains,
but then on winter nights, offers them words,
just words, that somehow keep them warm.

2017

Suspension

ces rois de l'azur, maladroits et honteux* – CHARLES BAUDELAIRE

How can you bear your gifts so heavily?
Aloft, you are the light-winged albatross.
Often, you're that mariner who wears it.
Suspend for once your disbelief.
Live the miracles that loft you free.

1983

* *these kings of the azure skies, awkward and ashamed*

Customs of the Day

How simple, how frugal a thing is happiness. – NIKOS KAZANTZAKIS

It's the end of the world as we know it, and I feel fine. – R. E. M.

Power's off! Gas heat too (electric thermostat).
Glazed roads all but impassable.

I put on coat, knit cap, scarf, gloves
to carry hatchet and handsaw
into that patch of woods behind my house.

Snowy ice squeaks, crunches
easily under my boot heels
along a bride-white path.

I break, chop, or saw up an armload
of cold, dry hardwood
and heft it home.

I set a frugal fire in my hearth to settle by,
recalling cans of beans on the pantry shelf,
knowing I can heat them if need be.

I try the phone: a silent landline.
No mail today, but wait – it's Sunday.
No neighbors I know of who need a thing.
Utter isolation here – and I feel just fine.

I turn myself by this fire
as I did by the hot coal stoves of my boyhood,
surveying my walls and my wood,
feeling sufficient unto this day.

Distant evening sun glosses
the cold cake frosting out my window.
Decorative candles in the house
quietly reclaim their ancient clout.

I should not talk so much about myself . . .

I pick one to light and read by,
something from my old friend *Walden,*
neglected like the beans all this time.
My eyes light randomly on these lines:

*To read well, that is, to read true books in a true spirit,
is a noble exercise,
and one that will task the reader more than any exercise
which the customs of the day esteem.*

Customs of the day indeed!
I feel closer to Henry's day tonight than I ever did.

What if I lost my bifocals and couldn't read,
or lost my sight – or even my mind!
Or what if I were riddled in this unaccustomed quiet
with regret, that worst disease – but no.

The rare euphoria instead,
this holy cell of warmth and light within
the greater cold and dark outside
(and yes, that universal darkness
reaching further than we know)
glistens eyes in candlelight.

And so, with little else to do, I sit secure,
still enough to be at peace,
to contemplate the variables that are down tonight,
the vital ones still serving every need.

I breathe. I meditate.
If I took that easy further leap
and prayed, this freezing Sunday evening,
luckily I'd have no need to wish for something more.

It would be instead
a prayer of gratitude.

2002

Bi-polarity

I thought I might even be the fire
where folk would gather
in welcome warmth and light.

Toast marshmallows maybe,
have heart-to-hearts,
fall asleep on blankets spread.

But I may blaze up unpredictably
to singe the unwary, swirl
lethal sparks onto anything flammable,

then sometimes die back down
to the sullen chill of darkness,
to embers that say only, *Go*.

I'll never know
where I get the fuel
or how I feed it to the flame

or even how I have the warmth
to be that fire,
instead of dozing by one.

197_

I should not talk so much about myself...

Good Intention

The best-laid plans gang aft agley – ROBERT BURNS

I meant to get work done today,
but here's this book I couldn't leave
and the afternoon so mild and free,
I chose the curved trunk of an oak
for a backrest and sat on the lawn
to read, though my mind drifted
with a brief, seasonal whisp of wind
that chose, in an impish way,
to flutter the pages to and fro
as if to say there wasn't a thing,
nothing at all to do just now,
except to breathe the summer air
and be alive for one more day.

2015

Euphoriacs

If I could only live at the pitch that is near madness
When everything is as it was in my childhood
Violent, vivid, and of infinite possibility . . . – RICHARD EBERHART

Don't bother to Google it.
I did and came up with a band
I'd never heard of.

Unlike maniacs or insomniacs,
we euphoriacs
aren't bat-shit crazy
or red-eyed for lack of sleep.

We just experience
these feelings of intense
excitement and happiness
a *lot*, as some have seen –

which can cause equally intense
feelings of *un*happiness
in those who'd rather not endure
such perennial good cheer.

A favorite ex of mine
once gave me a Christmas card
with a blind Frosty the Snowman
reaching into his stocking
and finding to his excitement
two eye-sized lumps of coal.
My friend thought I'd like it
since it always took too little
to make me happy.

You may have heard
someone, maybe me,
tell the one, also a Christmas story,
about two little boys, identical twins,

I should not talk so much about myself . . .

except that Billy was all optimist,
and his Eeyore of a brother Joey
just the opposite.*

Nobody's always up
of course, or always down like that.
Nobody never swings between those poles.

A true euphoriac, at best,
reaches lovely highs
that aren't exhausting
and never trigger interventions,
as well as the mildest lows,
more like lulls or respites,
which is just what my first life coach told me:

*Eventually with luck and effort
your lows will be higher
than your highs are now.*

When friends ask me
how I am, and I say,
Better by the minute!
I should probably be saying,
Better for the moment instead,
not assuming this flighty vessel
will always touch down smoothly
or ever reach such heights again.

But as they say,
only hopelessly average folk
have a nice day every day.

2019

*The little pessimist got many toys but didn't like any of them and was in a tearful rage on Christmas morning. When the little optimist twin opened his only gift, a sack of horse manure, he ran around exclaiming, "Oh boy, oh boy, there's gotta be a pony around here somewhere!" I've often quoted that kid.

Full Disclosure

Here's to the years I spent,
all of them actually,
but especially the ones
figuring out who it was I was,
who I thought I was becoming.

Here's to stolen hours hidden
in college library stacks
scanning suspected biographies
of men I thought might be
deviant, demonized like me.

Ah, this one never married,
that one had a traveling secretary,
another faced a scandal,
one was murdered
execution style.

I didn't learn it from Mom
who assured me instead
there was a little girl,
probably born already,
who would be *just right* for me.

There was truth there too,
and why regret the decade
and more I committed
to being a woman's man,
fathering sons with her?

My folks must have wondered though
when at four I asked for and got
my own dollhouse. It helped
arrange the fragile furniture
of a small world I thought was mine.

I should not talk so much about myself . . .

It was some challenge,
figuring out the facts.
Like Jesus, Dad never said
a word on the subject,
though he did urge me

to stop running away
from neighborhood bullies
who somehow knew me
in ways I never knew
myself back then.

*When that Billy Smith
tries to chase you home next time,
you stop, turn around,
just double up your fists,
and he'll mess in his pants.*

Here's to every ache,
every embarrassment,
every disgrace I endured
for falling far from the norms.
All of it got me here

to an actual world
where I thrive, know love,
enjoy the fulfilled self I am,
free among knowing friends
who, like me, gave up running.

2019

Holding On & Letting Go

This hand holds a pencil,
moves along the page, holding on, letting go,
allowing an adequate word, appropriate phrase to flow.
So it is with mind's slow motion,
so with every human movement,
holding on, letting go.

Afternoons I climbed
our grand magnolia tree,
hugged its hard, elephant skin
beneath its fragrant, milk-white blooms and glossy leaves,
straddled a low gray limb, inching outward to swing down
from hooked knees till I was hanging free,
fingers nearly touching the ground,
half holding on,
half letting go.

Then one year
came Death at our back door
to sweep my father's dust away.
My mother clung to me and cried,
the preacher prayed. I trembled at a plated coffin rail,
obstinately holding on, and with no understanding, letting go.
What blear-eyed childhood could not know is clear today:
He weathered his allotted years, as I do now,
meeting a partly-chosen fate,
holding on, letting go.

When, every fall,
the fair appeared in town,
I paid my way to ride the ferris wheel.
Defying fear, I learned to draw its giddy circles,
coolly holding on in constant breeze, and letting go.
I thrilled and reeled above kaleidoscopic tents and lights,
folk crowding the musical midway row on row.
I rose and fell with belly-rippling bravado,
spinning slow.

I should not talk so much about myself . . .

Countless other moments
live again, enlarged in meaning:
hands I held on summer evenings,
kisses blithely savored in convenient dark alcoves,
quick embraces sometimes nervous and uncertain –
so many varied ways to hold one close – or let one go.
And all those gallant, glad rehearsals led me on to one
and to an overwhelming question, posed and answered
at a plain white altar where friends and family rose:
marriage made by holding on
(unmade by letting go).

Predictably
with fond parental hands
we got and held our own,
till one by one they found their feet
and wandered off to places we never dreamed of going.
Every season of their own amazing growth marked our way:
Love them well, hold them close,
then let them go.

In all good conscience,
we may never know how far and well
our lives fare by following a subtle flow of something large,
something we call God or nature, while it still remains unnamed,
something in and over us that moves our breathing spirits,
moves by holding on
and letting go.

198_

What Ifs

I know that petty, nagging feeling:
Some other, finer life was freely offered,
but I wasn't paying attention that day.
Maybe I tossed a lucrative opportunity
out with a half-glanced handful of junk mail,
possibly even some ideal lover's appeal unread.

So I got this matter-of-fact life instead,
with all its acquiescence and compromise,
its facile comforts, ruts tugging me from bed
half-hearted on a steel-cold winter morning,
confident only that I've learned how to brew
a decent pot of coffee and grateful it's for two.

But what if this really *is* the life, practically
all I could have dreamed, had I but known,
instead of second-guessing all I was and am?
Not to change the subject much at all, but
what if, however many earth-like planets
are glimpsed where water and even life *might* be,

this, *this* tiny thriving place is the one oasis,
in all the cosmos where such life is – and us living it,
with our sturdy little cups filled over half-way,
with even enough at times to ease another's thirst,
this world where fate and choices make us
with all our tragi-comic doubts and graces?

2017

Best

But the best thing is to possess one's own soul in silence.
– D. H. LAWRENCE

Sometimes I discover myself
in the sanctum of a private joy.

Perhaps while Piaf is crooning
Non, je ne regrette rien,
I submit to a completeness
unpredictable, incomparable,
insusceptible to words.

It's then I realize,
all is truth and beauty here,
the immortality Keats knew
at midnight in an English garden
as a nightingale was singing.

Afterwards, eyes closed,
I sink deeply, deeply
toward a fathomless oblivion.
And in that dark appears a ring of light,
the circle circling everything

to celebrate the simple, calm,
sweet dream in the vast overmind
of the Unnamable.

1992

More Basic than Love

Know thyself; the unexamined life is not worth living. – SOCRATES

This state exists
far beyond lust,
beyond the truest
camaraderie,
beyond fiercest love –
the phenomenon
of waking identity,
touted by that sage
as a highest good:
Self-knowledge.

But loving oneself?
That risks narcissism.
Love's bridge joins two,
birds of a feather,
opposites attracted.
Self-helps advise us,
Love yourself.
How misguided!
I *am* myself and have to *be,*
for all it's worth.

I have to breathe
and feed and ambulate
and grow on into
the self I can become.
I do this living.
To be – assume
unique identity,
conscientiously –
love quails before
that mystery.

2007

*Fate chooses our relatives,
we choose our friends.*

– JACQUES DELILLE

Marcus

Think it no great thing to die after as many years as thou canst name rather than to-morrow. – MARCUS AURELIUS

My dear father's father's father,
Marcus Arealious Perryman
(That's how they spelled your middle name.):
You left a wife with four sons on the farm.

You marched off
with the Haralson Invincibles,
greener than a bush-league team,
to fight the damn' Yankees
up in Tennessee
where you fresh, brave,
frightened soldier-players
succumbed
to far less glorious evils than battle:
you, still young,
one of the legion dead.

Your cause was lost with you,
and now we can hardly grasp such fervor,
such pride, such obligation.

Imagine you, Marcus, born round 1830,
then turning twenty-one,
forsaking home
in the West Country
(laws of primogeniture
ignoring younger sons).

Your ship sailed,
from Portsmouth maybe, to Savannah,
then you discovered northwest Georgia,
a fertile land to settle, marry,
buy that farm,
begin to raise male heirs.

Fate chooses our relatives . . .

Imagine then you joined
that doomed rebellion,
to die in squalor and despair,
to die of measles and pneumonia
in 1862 – at 32.

Imagine you,
namesake
of a true philosopher-king,
come to such a servile end.

2012

Lena Shannon

My sad-eyed mother's mother
took in boarders to make ends meet
during that endless depression.

Still, she served up steaming dinners daily
for two bits when they were silver,
clinked into a sugar bowl that held no sugar.

*If you don't like it
you can eat at the Ritz*, she'd quip.
Oh, they liked it, all right.

And on rare mornings, her smile
was a welcome ray of sunshine
after soggy weeks of rain.

But when she sat and rocked
on her sunporch and sobbed
among litmus blooms of her african violets,

neighbors cringed
at her high tones
up and down North Avenue.

1974

Fate chooses our relatives . . .

Crossing Palms

If you can't make it to seventy by a comfortable route, don't go.
– MARK TWAIN

I met my mother's father
in passing only
before he passed for good
when I was eight.

It was my only live
encounter with the man,
he in his gold upholstered chair
backed by his bank of books.

He called me to his side
when I was maybe four.
He had me give him my hand,
raked an aged nail across my palm.

Oh, you have an excellent
lifeline here.
You'll have a fine,
long life, he prophesied.

Our only other crossing
hardly counts – he laid out
in a mortuary bed, inert,
ignoring me that time.

I hesitated at his side
until I felt my mother's
well-meant nudge
to take his waxen hand.

The ice of it chilled mine.
I drew back, shrinking
from the only human death
I've ever grasped that way.

These decades later, I just wish
he could have known
how well his wise prediction
is playing out these days.

Like the guy falling
and halfway down the side
of the Empire State building,
(but hopefully not too much like him)

I can honestly say at sixty-seven,
So far so good!

2012

Old Rhythms

Precious memories may remain, even of a bad home, if only the heart knows how to find what is precious. – FYODOR DOSTOEVSKY

Dad's evening hymn faints away
off the dusky verandah
where he rocked and hummed
to himself, sometimes

to me splayed across his lap,
bottom cupped in his calloused hand,
another one patting time
on my innocent back,

his labored breaths
at my ear breaking
from his heaving chest
into a rumbling bass refrain:

When we all . . . get to hea-ven,
What a won-der-ful day it will be . . . .

Long, thin legs pumping,
shoe soles tapping,
rocker bows riding
the rain-worn boards beneath us,

carrying us both in that rocker
to guaranteed glory.
Or, failing that,
rocking me at least

into sweet summer oblivion
to the see-saw counterpoint
of choral katydids
zinging out in the red oak trees.

1986

Salty Irreverence

My fabled aunt Mildred,
dubbed by me a fairy godmother,
nevertheless cursed like a sailor.

Eager learner that I was,
she taught me well
the swearing she used,
voiced in exasperation,
sometimes at my expense:

Dammit to hell, Donny!

Colorful variations included
Damn and blast!
and, my favorite, *Hell's bells!*
not that I was thrilled
when it was fired at me
in the awkward moment
of some misdemeanor.

She'd already taught me
that first trick of poetry,
challenging me, out for a ride
in her car one day,

*I'll give you a dime
if you make me a rhyme.*

My response, at age four maybe,
was, *Give me a nickel
and I'll give you a pickle,*
which evidently pleased her.
I was already a wannabe poet.

But her profanity was to me
her most fascinating trait,
if not to my more staid elders.

Fate chooses our relatives . . .

Mother overheard me practicing
Hell's bells! loud and clear
one afternoon when I thought
no one was within earshot.
I came out of that experience
just shy of a whipping.

With Mildred as mentor though,
I was pretty much incorrigible.
Mother dragging me
to that rural Baptist church
where the preacher grew red-faced
and sobbed in the pulpit against the world
and all its wrong did not convert me,
despite the beauty of the hymns we sang.

I preferred Mildred's parodies:

At the cross, at the cross
where I smoked my first cigar
and the burden of my heart rolled away.
It was there by chance
I tore my Sunday pants,
and now I have to wear them every day,
and then her dramatic, low-pitched refrain:
Every daaay!

She taught me a funny
if irreverent string
of spoonerisms too
about a nervous usher
on his first Sunday morning:

Mardon me, Padam,
I believe you're occupuing the wrong pie.
May I sow you to another sheet
or will you return tonight
when the service will be howled
in the hell below?

She shared with me
that salty side of herself
that she spared
through professional restraint
the fourth-graders she taught
for thirty-five years,
telling them once,

*Now when that bell rings
don't all of you
get up and mash dadly out that door,*
which also got a laugh,
though on that occasion
it was a slip of the tongue.

She saved her best intentional stuff for me.

2018

Familiarity

for my elders

O tempora o mores – *CICERO*

Mother used to say it,
just as it was said to her,
along with her mother's warning
to be home from skating neighborhood sidewalks
before the gas streetlamps were lit:

Familiarity breeds contempt.

A few years after she got that warning,
in the teens of World War One,
a young cavalryman borrowed horses
from the Army stables in Atlanta
and took my not-yet-mother out to ride.

As they waited at a railroad crossing,
she seated modestly side-saddle,
a locomotive came huffing down the track.
Her horse reared, and the young man gallantly
(opportunistically, I would bet)
hopped down just in time to catch her,
as she slid off into his capable (welcoming) arms.

I was thrilled, she confessed to me
with a faraway gaze, decades after the fact,
betraying no contempt over that familiarity.

I'll swear that my father, a career Navy man,
renting a room in her parents' home on North Avenue
a few years after that war, was her first – and only,
though she survived him by two loyal decades.

He admitted to her she was not *his* first,
But I never went with a virgin, he quaintly claimed!
He even shared a story about a trick

his Navy buddies tried to play on him once
when their ship was docked at Naples, Italy,
during that same Great War.

A Georgia country boy
with a mother who also scorned undue familiarity,
he had a reputation among the sailors as a prude,
so they fixed him up a blind date – with a prostitute.

When he called on her and realized what they'd done,
he bought her a corsage, took her to dinner and the opera,
left her at the brothel door with a kiss – on her hand, mind you –
and sent her a box of candy the next day.

Back aboard ship, his horrified buddies marveled
how he could have been such a fool.
Perryman, she was a whore!
We spent good money on her,
they must have complained.

His response? at least the one I got via my mother:

I knew she was no lady.
I treated her like one anyway,
because I'm a gentleman.

My mother became *his* lady –
but only after a proper wedding
officiated by her beloved Uncle Frank, a Methodist minister,
in the family home where Dad had been a boarder.

The night before, she asked her mother,
What will we do on our wedding night?

He will show you, she assured her naive daughter.

After their vows and all the goodbyes,
they left to take the train cross-country to Seattle,
Dad's next duty station.
Before they boarded, a light rain began.

Fate chooses our relatives . . .

She opened her matching parasol,
and a tell-tale shower of rice scattered from inside,
embarrassing her discreet new husband,
she recalled to me with a laugh.

Chugging blissfully along,
they steamed past Pike's Peak, *snow-capped*, she wrote
in her new leather-bound diary with the little lock,
and then this:

The West certainly does inspire love!

He added his comment in yeoman's shorthand
along the margin, untranslated to this day.

A few months later,
together on their own in their first home,
she confessed to that diary,
Our first real spat. It was all my fault.

There were enough familiar good times too,
and as far as their love-life went,
she shocked me once, long after his demise,
with this sweet revelation:

Your father always made sure I was satisfied.

Another of my mother's learned advisories,
There's safety in numbers, clearly meant
that when a boy and a girl are off to themselves
they're more likely to get into trouble.

Not long into her widowhood,
she gave me a record-player for Christmas
with an LP that happened to include the song,
Wake up, Little Susie!

When I played it the first time,
she stood there, taking in the lyrics,
forearms crossed over her buttoned bodice.

You'll recall the song if you're of a certain age –
all about falling asleep on an innocent date at the drive-in,
years after chaperones (and horses) had been the thing.
The boy's panic was palpable:

The movie wasn't so hot. It didn't have much of a plot.
It's four o'clock, our goose is cooked, our reputation is shot!
What're we gonna tell your mama?
What're we gonna tell your pa?
What're we gonna tell our friends when they say, "Ooo la la"?

My mother's judgment of that song was succinct and final:

That's suggestive, she declared and left me to my music.

Behaviors and cautionary tales evolve as years go by.
Our ideas of acceptable familiarity have relaxed indeed,
even though we still believe, just as my parents did,
that we risk in our familiarizing
not just contempt, but love.

2017

The Widow

She always used to say,
*God never sends us more
than we can stand.*

And believing that
saw her through
numerous domestic crises.

Sweltering Sunday afternoons
she rocked bereaved
on those old boards
of that weathered verandah,
with a *Woman's Home Companion* for a fan.

In freezing January dark,
she lay tensed and sleepless
as pipes threatened to freeze and crack
under the icy linoleum.

She suffered vague
respiratory ailments
her grown-up children
in cities miles away
could never quite imagine,

suffered more familiar heartbreaks
than I would care
to recollect or name,

especially that last, literal one
that left her really broken,
exhausted as a busted leather bellows,

by which time I'd begun to figure for myself
what her dark saying meant anyway.

1977

Heart of Gold

Stella Elizabeth Shannon Perryman
(October 7, 1903 – November 16, 1977)

My mother's deeds were modest.
She was rarely proud or bold.
The flesh proved all too fragile –
but her heart was gold.

The subtle transformation
wasn't done till she was old.
While her hair was turning silver,
her heart was turning gold.

I saw her creasing wrinkles,
saw her wide eyes roll,
saw it fully afterwards –
her heart had turned to gold.

I live with this awareness:
Her folded arms are cold,
but in my beating heart I keep
a mother's heart of gold.

1978

Weather Report

Remember,
when leaves darken and let go
to fall in dead confusion with the snow;

remember,
when this landscape dozes like the bears
in the gloomy refuge of their lairs;

remember,
when fragile windowpanes
weep blindly in a frigid rain:

despite foul dealings
of any outside weather,
you and I, Love, have an inside chance

for warm delights and fairest weather
for the weekend –
and forever?

1969

Winter Aubade

Black night pales
to a motionless
pink explosion
lighting eastern sky
along its rim.

Oaks stand grim
in frozen air.
An isolated car
negotiates the street
in clinging chains.

Frost on panes
distorts a spectacle
of winter dawn
through sleep-
encumbered eyes.

He doesn't rise.
He burrows back
in the animal comfort
of their marriage,
holding her warm side.

197_

Fate chooses our relatives . . .

Trinity

for Jeff

The child is father of the man. – WILLIAM WORDSWORTH

This I dreamed when you were born:

My father dead,
laid at length on an icy slab,
gaunt and hopeless
like our grief,
spectral pale, eyes sealed,
linen about his loin,
my mother's eyes aglaze.

Supine person, in death epitomized:
Christ again, down from his hard crossing.

Then, before my widening gaze,
his blue breast rose.

He's alive, I whispered.
No, he's gone, my mother cried.

Not to be denied,
I reached down with young, insistent arms
to raise him up.

I saw a living face,
eyes trained on me,
the clearest incarnation
of you, my new-born son.

1970

For My Niece, Graduating High School

When you go, Carole,
we say to the loving ghost of girlhood that lingers in you,
don't forget the barefoot grass of magic springtime sunrise,
or the morning-glory yards of home you rode your happy
    bright new bike around in, and around again in,
or that small summer beach of tiny scuttling fiddler crabs
    that scared you off your shepherd feet.
Remember souvenirs of silly friends and movies, wallet
    photos, ticket stubs, the tips of budding loves,
star-stud nights in princess gowns, perspiring palms, floral
    tunes and tempos all your own.
Don't forget the velvet tongues and crystal eyes that sought and
    taught what only starting lovers learn.
Don't forget, beyond such recollections, life's joy that finds
    its winning way (and will) in you,
or how to make those lilting waves of laughter light your lovely
    face.
Don't forget all those who've loved you.
Don't forget how much we do.

1974

Home Scenes

Scott tunnels under the covers,
his head an expectant bump of spread
at the foot of our double bed.
He's hiding out.
But he wants very much to be found
by monster-daddy
who'll snarl and scare him good.
I pounce on squeals
to feel his face grimacing, grinning.

Jeff's a Peter-Paul-and-Mary man.
He hugs his guitar's neck
and all alone he croons along
with every sad and lovely tune
as one by one the scratchy records spin
songs about a lemon tree,
a magic dragon in the sea.
His smiling mother motions me
to peek with her around the door at him.

1976

Fathers Wake

for Jeff and Scott

The raucous evening done,
the paddled boys abed,
contritely now I come
to cup each sleeping head.

My moonlit presence here
may lightly jar a dream,
but I must rest my fear,
so dead asleep they seem.

1978

Pretender

I spoke you love. I wrote you love –
everything from sweet nothings to sonnets.
I gave you extemporaneous elaborations
on the uniqueness and value of our love,
how others who knew us were envious.
I gift-wrapped for you Klimt images
of women kissed and held by loving men,
took you to see *Zhivago*, and *Camelot*,
and Zeffirelli's *Romeo and Juliet*,
read you the balcony scene again afterwards.
I played the Beatles for you, and Stravinsky,
gave you volumes of passionate poetry,
all inscribed with loving words from me.
I made love with you in every way I knew.

But oh no, you had to have the real thing.

1981

Endgame

Little has changed really.
She still shifts mechanically
the lifeless kitchen pans.
He still rocks in a room apart
and reads in a wreath of smoke.

At least there are no lies.

They still wake for morning moments
over toast, preserves, and coffee,
one milk and sugar, one just sweet'n low.
Ruddy embers of loving glow
still in their shifting eyes.

1982

The Treehouse

for Jeff and Scott

It blossomed for you in a backyard tree:
two stories, trap doors, ladders, walls, shelves,
awnings on windows with hinged shutters,
and through it all the indulgent maple
threading its trunk and limbs freely skyward.

Even before I'd finished the project,
it was your fortress, rocket ship, haven
for braving balmy July nights
above the crickets, amid the frogs and katydids.

The kid-sized second-floor balcony was
a vantage point beneath the leaves and stars.
Painted top to bottom a camo of green,
it was one clear-cut accomplishment at least.

But it wasn't designed just to please you.
I had agreed to leave.
The treehouse was a final consolation.
I added a third-floor cupola, tinned the roofs,
and finished off my pleasurable folly.

Call it a memento, a father's souvenir.

1982

Summer Inspiration

for Scott

Cedar Key, Florida, summer 1984

Heat's oppressive,
and I can't write a decent word.

I veg in my tiny tower
of worn white clapboards
under sun-hot tin.
My senses dulled,
determination fizzled,
I'm dozing, headachy.

Suddenly this twelve-year-old
rushes in, slamming the screen,
hefting a sweating bucket of icy water
that holds, just barely,
one massive speckled trout.

Omigod, Dad, you shoulda seen him
floppin' in the cast net when I pulled him up!

Energized,
I clean your prize,
we two admiring
the glistening innards,
the sheer bulk of the filets.

You slice up potatoes for fries
and ask me to make hushpuppies.

As we sit to eat, I watch you
glug ketchup onto your plate.

I savor how we each earned our dinner,
you with your proud catch, I with mine.

Fate chooses our relatives . . .

Mildred's Garden

Florida birds are splashing
under twisted live-oak limbs.
Through my bedroom window
trickle their bright hymns.

Sunlight shafts magnolia
in a glaze of gold on green.
Box turtles rustle
under the leaves unseen.

My maiden aunt still tends
this Eden where I wake.
Her eighty-seasons' wisdom?
Every garden has a snake.

1984

Local Colors

That fairy-godmother aunt was a proud van Gogh
boldly daubing her retirement in provincial Florida
sunlight with her favorite color – yellow.
For her flower creations she grew real flowers,

her garden an orderly riot, a sane daydream:
always yellow, always her second favorite, green,
but more: cobalt blues, snowflake jasmine, day-glo
zinnias, pink shrimp plants, bride-white gardenias.

It was a frugal scene: spade propped beside a door,
green garden hose coiled by the walk she'd paved,
pepper plants in coffee cans sprouting minute reds
ready to be set out and well soaked soon.

She painted her whole house yellow
with green trim – a gigantic bright sunflower
blooming amid the others. Even the last
little car I found for her, a Gremlin – shiny yellow.

Inside that cheerful cottage she painted
a wee green guest room with, yes, a yellow chair
beside a narrow wooden bed under
a low, slant ceiling with a rain spot or two.

And as she rocked away the screened-in, golden
evenings of her feisty, old-maid eighties,
she painted for me all the scenes she'd lived or dreamed,
brighter and brighter as the dark came on.

1992

Fate chooses our relatives . . .

Just Don't Set Fire to the House!

for Jack and Kate and Sam, from Papa, spring 2006

If you should lose my favorite pen
or leave my flashlight lit
or eat up all the M&M's
or even yell a bit,
if you forgot your ABC's
or where you left your shoe
or how to wait while others speak,
I will still love you.

If you threw up on my white shirt
or spilled a glass of juice
all down inside the VCR
or let the hamster loose
or even smacked your brother hard
or thought up something new
to drive us grown-ups up the wall,
I would still love you.

If beds bounced out of your back door
and sofas did a dance,
if your closet opened wide
and dumped out all your pants,
if all your toys crashed down the stairs
and bikes came flying through
your bedroom window while you slept,
I promise, I'd love you.

If skies turned green and trees turned blue
and the moon turned chocolate brown,
if jellyfish got arms and legs
and birds perched upside down,
if bears grew fins and fish grew fur
and rocks all turned to goo,
if everything went nuts at once,
You *know* I'd still love you!

For Jessi & Michael on Your Wedding Day

Let me not to the marriage of true minds
admit impediments: love is not love
which alters . . . .
Oh, no; it is an ever-fixed mark,
That looks on tempests, and is never shaken. – WILLIAM SHAKESPEARE

The Bard wrote love lasts forever.
Otherwise it isn't real.
He understood true love is never
just some passing urge we feel.

However hard life's storms may blow,
wherever earthly fortunes lie,
whatever trials we undergo,
authentic love does not die.

So let that be our wish for you,
Jessi, Michael, standing here
to vow that you will each be true
to one another all your years.

And more than wishing, let us say
we know you have a lovely chance
to celebrate, not just this day,
but for a lifetime of romance.

The honest work you've done so far
to make your lives exemplary
suggests that there should be no bar
to what your future lives can be.

If we could promise you blue skies
with not a dark cloud in your way,
you know we would. But let us try
to share now all we hope and pray:

The integrity you've shown already
and this love that you have vowed

will set you on a course so steady
you'll out-weather any cloud.

So show the world and show yourselves
what married bliss is meant to be,
from the ringing of your wedding bells
through years of lasting harmony.

We thank you both for this glad sight
of two young lovers, enthralled and thrilled.
And here's more proof Shakespeare was right:
We love you and we always will.

2012

*Friendship is born
at the moment when one
person says to another:
What! You too? I thought
I was the only one.*

– C. S. LEWIS

Thank You, Miss Edith

We found the Georgia apples you left at our door.
We could imagine you stooping to reach the floor,
easing the sack down carefully, leaving them there.
They were tasty, sweet – almost as sweet as your care.

The easiest, simplest things are always the best,
but often, for dubious reasons, ignored for the rest.
A nation that rockets men off to the moon and back
should remember . . . but never mind, I'm getting off my track.

My starting intention was purely and plainly to say
it was so thoughtful of you, leaving apples that way;
but poets can be so effusively grateful at times
we try to thank neighbors with lines of pentameter rhymes.

197_

Song for a Swan

the lady who lived downstairs

If only this damnable dying
muffling your rare goodness
to a ghostly whisper now
could summon from my young mind,
innocent as it must be of the awful riddle,
some song commensurate
to your fine life, Bess Swann.

You were a woman of handsome grace.
The azure of your eyes reflected heavens.
Love was a word you rarely had to use.
Now we have a shadow of all you were.

Discreetly, one floor up from you,
we guess the death-dance your poor frame endures.
You who lofted Sunday hymns above the rest,
put candy on your door-wreath for our boys.

What can I say of your decent deeds
as you slip wordlessly away?

First it took your lyric voice;
now it casually takes you.
Such loss deserves a better eulogy,
but my voice falters too. . . .

197_

Friend

for Mark

Let us swear an oath, and keep it with an equal mind,
In the hollow Lotus-land to live and lie reclined
On the hills like Gods together, careless of mankind.
– ALFRED LORD TENNYSON

As we wind another way
among the earthy ruts
of muddling men, day on day,

remember once we rested
in a sunlit mountain meadow
couched on a gradual green.

It was an Appalachian spring.
We spied on browsing deer.

Through our own lenses
and through wider lenses still,
we surveyed the quilted landscape
from a loft of cloudless blue.

But what survives here
in the traffic's metal press?
What's left for minds that linger on such scenes,
that even once slowed to an easy rhythm,
miles from the nearest man-made thing?

Remember our taste for yellow cheese,
sips of pale Chablis from a leather bota,
the touch of a hand on sunlit shoulder,
an honest word of praise.

Tomorrow squint the mind
and see it all again.

197_

Friendship is born at the moment . . .

Night Letter

for Mark

Invisible warm rain's falling
round these open windows.
It's one a.m. A throb of rain
accumulates to a steady roar,
rises and offers to dampen
gold curtains, tile floor,
then patters gently down again.

So much here is green:
dieffenbachia, philodendron,
a domesticated rain forest
of barely dripping leaves,
and an old oil lamp
assuming its saffron glow
by which to write lines
I know you'll understand.

197_

Letter Home

The wanderer does not bring from the mountain-slope a handful of earth to the valley, inexpressible earth, but only a word he has chosen.
– ERICH MARIA RILKE

I'm standing here in the surf this summer evening,
as waves wash flatly about my ankles,
eating away the sand beneath my toes.
Blowing ashore is a night wind off the bay.
But you'll never have been here now,
never have known it quite this way.

You'll not have heard this roar tonight
at the shoreline – a long, monotonous, moaning roar,
never have breathed in this steady breeze,
salty and bracing, that I breathe as I stroll near the surf.
You'll miss the particular crunch of the dry beach sand.
It squeaks now warmly, rhythmically under my heels.

Words never deliver such things: whatever
that blinking green light, rocking out
on the channel buoy, seems to be saying,
what those sea clouds suggest as they drift
past a pearlescent visage of moon.
There's no true communion, no ultimate sharing.

But I go on marshalling images and pondering
more ways to tell you, dear friend of my heart,
that the waves in the surf tonight did moan
as they bubbled the slushy sand at my feet,
and a warm night wind ran easily shoreward,
slipping milky cloud streamers across a taciturn moon,

while that buoy just rocked right on in the channel,
revealing more than any words could ever say.

197_

Getting to Heaven

St. Joseph Peninsula, Florida, April 18-20, 2003

A Book of Verses underneath the Bough,
A Jug of Wine, a Loaf of Bread - and Thou
  Beside me singing in the Wilderness –
Oh, Wilderness were Paradise enow!
– OMAR KAYYAM/EDWARD FITZGERALD

If and when I gain those fabled gates,
I'll know the lay of that land:

It might be a salt-white, shell-strewn beach
nudging a lemonade sea under kind sun
where I'll lounge safe in shade and rosy,
sheltered under a pitched green tarp
with a dozen lazy pals like you,
bantering easily, tipping up the rum.

Or should I arrive in the dark, weary
under that laughable load
I schlep with me everywhere I go,
I will find feasting, fellowship, and laughter
by a crackling fire under twisting pines
in a maritime world where a motherly
milk-white moon guards from on high.

We'll trade rollicking bearhugs
and tease with each other again,
bold and shy by turns.

We'll re-live so idyllic a weekend
that another rosy Dawn will swoon
and weep empathetic tears onto our tents –
as she really did that Saturday morning.

We'll splash and dive and soak ourselves again
at the mere edge of a vast, bracing
expanse of innocent ocean
that constantly bathes our almost-island.

And till I do get in those gates,
whatever gates I finally reach,
Well, my friends,
I'll trust my memories
of you, no matter where we go,
and have a heaven anyway.

Song for Solomon

You are old, Father William, the young man said. – LEWIS CARROLL

So you say I'm growing old – indeed,
that finest loving friends have left me – yes,
that age may prove a test of chronic need,
its trials worse than anyone might guess.

Then I'll invite what comes; I'll live to see
what troubles lurk ahead, what chance and luck
may haply visit on the likes of me.
And then I trust some innate grace – or pluck –

will see me through the coming tribulations.
But if you would suggest that this is all
a fruitless journey ending in frustration,
that I'll have lost life's struggle when I fall,

I'll say to you, *Oh, no, I've clearly won*:
I've had afternoons with Solomon.

2006

Haircuts

I visit the old-fashioned barber shop
with the patriotic red-white-blue pole
turning outside in the local strip mall.

$12 instead of the $15 at Smart Cuts,
and a lot like the small-town shop
where I got mine cut fifty years ago
for seventy-five cents (dollar for a flat-top,
but not in the family budget back then).

One of two Hispanic men usually cuts it.
As he rose to greet and point me to his chair,
I tell him, *Don't worry about getting it too short.*

He says, *Yes, this summer weather is hot and will get hotter.*

Thank heaven for air conditioning, I say
and chuckle with him how we never had it growing up
(already more words than we'd ever ventured before).

How old are you? he asks.

56, I tell him.

Well, he smiles, turning off his trimmer,
I am 62, so I remember even farther back than you.
I notice then how good his English sounds.

Next we talk about the wildfires out West.
He says they need a better way to fight them,
as if a nation so rich should have one by now.

I mention nine miners saved in Pennsylvania last week.
What a great thing that was, we agree.

He speaks of his son in Santo Domingo
who called the night before,

Friendship is born at the moment . . .

their talk interrupted by the six-year-old saying
(according to my friend's translation)
*Tell Papi to send you some money, Daddy,
so you can get me a computer.*

We laugh at how the times have changed.
The radio's playing Peter Paul and Mary.
That's an old one, I suggest.

Yes, he agrees, pausing his trimmer again,
all the best songs are old ones now.

Then for the first time
since I've been going there,
he brushes lather round my ears
and all along the nape of my neck,
then deftly slides away the hairs with a straight razor,
towels me dry, dusts me off with his powdered brush,
and like a matador whisks off the cloth
to let me up.

I give him a ten and a five and tell him it's a great job.
He thanks me, we shake firmly and grin our goodbyes.
I stroll out, energized.

Tonight in the tub
I run my hand up the back of my neck,
tingling the short bristles.

Suddenly I'm a ten-year-old
with my first one-dollar flat-top.

2002

Gardenias

for Anita

Graced with such good friends,
I never had a better one than you.

I pinched one gardenia daily,
from an abundant bush
outside the rehab center
where you lay in gradual decline.

We savored each reliable aroma.

One day, I told you,
*I may be in a bed this way,
and my great comfort then
will be my thoughts of you – your courage.*

I'll be right there,
was your immediate answer,
unhesitating, certain.

No finer scent or recollection
than emanates from such sweet blooms.

A whole bowl of them sits now,
aroma filling the air in our living room.

I'm healthy, happy,
evidently nowhere near
a final bed of pain, but still,

without a shred of superstition,
with hardly any thought at all,
I hear you say so clearly,
I'm right here.

2013

Plight*

Let me not to the marriage of true minds
Admit impediments. – WILLIAM SHAKESPEARE

Thus, though we cannot make our sun
Stand still, yet we will make him run. – ANDREW MARVELL

Please, stay a little longer than you would.
We have more lusty jokes and tales to tell,
and I'll find even better ones, I swear,
to rock you with the raucous belly laugh
I always long to hear from happy you.
We'll have more food, more wine, more music, yes,
more intimacies too, more truths to tell.
Ah, more of everything but strength and time.
Grudging thanks for warning wiser me
of what may come – but like a foolish boy,
I wring and pace. I agonize and plead.
Selfish? Sure, and weak perhaps, to cling.
Your peace, though, weary patron, finest friend,
will be my coldest, hardest comfort here.
When in my brimming heart I hold you still,
Will it be balm that you did love me? Yes.
But will it heal such an overwhelming wound?
That too may one day be, but now I have
a face no longer young, all wrenched and wet,
almost bereaved before bereavement. I
who make great mirth of witty words and live
to celebrate life's skylark ecstasies,
then fall, am falling wordless now – and yet,
I love you, love you. What else can I say –
but stay awhile, oh please. . . .

*I sent this to my oldest, best friend, Bob, in the 1990's after he'd suggested that he might not live much longer after his bypass surgery. He did though, more than twenty years, so I did get my wish.

Scrabble Buddies

for Esther and Stan

We've been quarantined so long
now, neither of us could say
for sure who won the last game,
what treat you brought to share,
or if it was one or both of you that day.

We shook hands freely, hugged hello,
lips touched! We hugged goodbye.
How could we have guessed our
easy privilege was on such short supply,
not ours to have again for one long year?

We've lost the thoughts we shared
in conversation, looked-up words
we found to play. Imagine how
we visited together, friends, nonchalant,
with never a thought of this contagion.

Our space conscribed, our free time
stretched to such a dull monotony
of caution, safe routine, delay;
grudgingly we wait for some all-clear
that might let us resume our play.

2020

For the Woman at the Waffle House

September 7, 2019

I wanted my favorite breakfast fix,
so I ordered the cheese and eggs,
then realized I'd left my cellphone
in the car and was just there,
alone with my ruminations.

Then you came in
with your bespectacled little boy
and took a seat by me.
I thought again how rare it is
that we talk to each other
the way we used to do
before all the modern distractions –
back when we'd speak more freely,
exchanging pleasantries
with someone by us at a counter,

back when we rocked on porches
and chatted with neighbors
who came by unannounced,
instead of being hermetically sealed
inside electrically conditioned air
we've learned to need,
eyes hypnotized by a TV screen.

I decided right then I'd reach out,
rehearsed my opening gambit,
not wanting to be a bother
or seem like some creep on the make,
just to be the amiable old gent
as I often manage to be.

When I looked over, though,
you were checking your cellphone,
and for that matter

Friendship is born at the moment . . .

your owlish little fellow
was glued to his small screen too –
mesmerized by fluffy bunny rabbits
hopping around the animated scene.

I smiled philosophically,
resumed my private thoughts –
but then you put your phone aside,
prompting me to wonder again
if we might still converse,
maybe set a good example
of cheerful geniality
in this modern reign of strangers.
Maybe it was because you were nice-
looking, well-dressed, intelligent,
being an attentive mother too.

Then you ordered the cheese and eggs,
giving me a better opening
than *Do you come here often?*
So I asked if you always ordered those.
You smiled and said you did.
We wondered then
if we were typical customers.
You even asked the server
who said, *No, it's usually eggs over medium.*
We smiled like a pair of renegades,
none of which matters at all,
except that we'd made these overtures.

I paused to give you a break
but almost laughed when you said it:
Do you come here a lot?

OK, I thought, *don't take this as license
to bend her ear all morning*,
flaming extrovert that I often am.
But of course I said *Yes*,
and then we hit our stride.

Talk about cellphones and social media
(tools not so bad as people claim)
how the first crank telephones jangled
on walls of homes, intruding
on old-fashioned peace and privacy.

Then we agreed how nice it is to connect
with folks – and these days on Facebook,
some of them from a remote childhood
we never thought we'd visit again.

When you mentioned high-school friends
you've found that way years later,
I said I'd been a high school teacher
and that a number of former students
and I had reconnected on-line
in a new, egalitarian way.

Then you said you monitored
your kid's screen time, adding,
*Although this little one
doesn't care much about sports,
he's a whiz with computers
and I think I should encourage that.*

Of course, I agreed, and then
we were on to parenting skills and perils.
I enjoyed helping raise my boys, I offered,
*but I can look back now and see
mistakes I made in ignorance and inexperience.*

Oh me too, you readily agreed,
sounding almost relieved.

So I added what I'd read in a book
when the boys were young:
*We all set out to be great parents,
but if we end up being good-enough ones,
we've done our jobs respectably.*

I'm sure you were a great one,
was your generous reply,
and I didn't care to correct you,
accepting the compliment instead.

Well, by then you and I
were done with our breakfast
and ready to pay up and leave,
which we did, with friendly good-byes.

Dear woman, though I never got your name,
thank you for taking a seat by mine today.

Love takes off the masks that we fear we cannot live without and know we cannot live within.

– JAMES BALDWIN

Maxims

A wise old woman
advised me once,
*There are those that love
and those that don't.*

Is it really that stark? I wondered.
Well, she added,
*Many are learning how,
and some may be forgetting.*

2012

Song

Some say the world will end in fire,
Some say in ice. – ROBERT FROST

The inching miracle,
that cramped, frigid
flesh-soul still survives,
is song for glad singing.

Ice crystallizes, forms
hate-filled on warmth's effort,
would enclose, freeze all,
but no, love grows.

197_

Afterglow

This having been once, though once only . . . can it ever be blotted out?
– RANIER MARIA RILKE

In mildest gauze of moonlight
these luminescent limbs
blended amid bedclothes
where we unclothèd lay,
two pale, marbled figures
in limpid pools of moonlight,
lingering after our first
carefree play.

In clearer light than twilight,
little moons, our eyes,
curved upward to the sky
and to each other too
in wordless fascination.
Blue-white moonlight
drenched us utterly.
All was still and true.

But then you moved, and I
saw cloud shadows slipping by,
blue curtains closing down
the plainest scene of all.
Did we imagine in such limelight
we might have our way,
that time would take no toll?

Tonight I know too well,
leaning chilled by a concrete wall
on a bluer, moonless night,
collar clutched against the cold,
that it was afterglow
that briefly held us so.

1983

Sundown on Cedar Key

Sky's black and blue and bloody,
silhouetting tangled live oak limbs.

Somewhere out there frogs and bugs
are sawing away in predetermined lust.

I lounge on a bed in the window breeze
reading D. H. Lawrence by lamplight.

The poor fisherman next door's been catching it
from his exasperated wife for hours:

Don't gimme any more a ya goddam excuses!
she fairly screams.

Words from the page saw at me in tandem:
Perfect love is an absurdity.

197_

Unfound Lover

Unfound brother, lover, friend,
where might you yet be discovered?
Where are your marbled fingers
with their knowing touch and twitch
along my cringing neck
to gentle me, settle me back
into this thin, taut skin?
Where are your prismatic eyes,
your winks and curls about the lip
where all the ironies take form?
Where are our fierce holds and thrusts
and midnight consummations
with all the bruising kisses?

Because I am so ready,
because these tilting paths and lanes
and broad, whizzing avenues of wondering
and pain and ecstasy
are finally teaching me balance,
teaching me ease of this flesh,
these hidden bones.
And because we have so much to share:
the tacit understandings,
the cool rocks to sit on in the river,
the memories to be redeemed,
the sentimental bits of song
I'll sing for your amusement,
the ways we'll blend our bodies
in the bliss of dreamless sleep.
What a trove of treasures!
Want them, unfound brother, lover, friend –
and bring your own for me.

1988

How It Could Happen

He just might appear
at some Saturday Midtown party
I didn't really want to attend,
laughing good-naturedly with me
over the very same appetizer
we each reach for at once.

And I could suddenly wonder
how I got that near a handsome man
without noticing his appeal –
raven hair, golden skin, perhaps;
coal-dark eyes, curves of muscle
beneath his sweater and jeans;
clothes just snug enough,
not too revealing.

Maybe as our focus slipped
from food to other topics,
I'd come to see I needn't weigh my words.
Half an hour of easy conversation
could reveal some common themes:
movies, city life, wilderness retreats,
new music, poetry.
I might decide to tell him candidly,
You're charming me,
but I don't sense you trying to
or feel I have to try hard either.

My thought as well, he might agree
with an off-hand smile and chuckle.

Maybe I'd steal a look
into the lenses of his eyes,
wondering again whether people
can tell when you're doing that,
taking them totally in.

But maybe he'd meet my gaze
just long enough to suggest
he's scoping me that way too.

This time maybe I wouldn't shift
mechanically into a nervous act,
and he wouldn't start to fidget
or avert his captivating eyes,
neither of us betraying a sign
of needing to mingle away.

So now I'm torn between a wish
to cut him from this herd,
corral him well away somewhere –
or continue to savor with him
our easy conversation.

Penny for your thoughts,
he could say, catching me.

How much time do you have? I'd ask.

Could be a lot, he'd say. *And you?*

Maybe a whole lot,
I'd tell him with a goofy grin,
feeling oddly shy, if not prophetic,
as all the lucky indications
keep suggesting he's as pleased to be
with me as I with him.

Now where does it go from here?
Do we say our goodbyes to others
early on, go build us a fire
to bask at its cozy radiance,
continuing our acquaintance?

Maybe we make that escape.
Maybe we head for home,

either to his place or to mine,
to build that blaze and keep it going,
lounging lazy in its flickers.

Maybe we even fall asleep,
our weary limbs akimbo,
until the edge of morning sunrise
brightens the closed window blinds
as the radio keeps oozing out the oldies
we chose for background all night long.

And then what happens –
do we make ourselves some coffee,
then go for brunch at a quiet
little gay-friendly café?

Do we then sail right on through
an impromptu and blissful weekend –
or would some obligation intervene –
his commitment to an evening
church service possibly,
or my Sunday-evening plans
with some familiar flame
who's still a friend?

And either way, do we meet again,
only to find that our infatuation's
ebbing, that we have that old feeling
we don't want more time together,
that we'd just prefer to taper off
before it gets all complicated?

Or do we discover instead,
we aren't on each other's nerves,
haven't done with our fun together yet?

Do we possibly move on
with little effort from occasional dates
to spontaneous times together,

with or without the intimacy,
which, by the way, remains
lovely as a secret swimming
hole, shaded in deep, green woods
from strangers' eyes and July heat?

Maybe I catch myself humming
an old tune driving to see him again,
and then recall the words with a smile:

I've grown accustomed to your face. . . .

Or maybe I'd slide in an old CD
and really get, for the first time,
the poignance of Elton's song:

In the moment that you love someone. . . .

But then how long
before we begin to display
those inevitable kinks and quirks –
like my excessive laughter
or his resonant snoring,
like his lingering fascination
with his last lover's wit
or my awful dread that I'm going
to screw this up somehow?

Maybe I just lose my patience
with the fact that he's not out
to his parents yet, for god's sake.
Maybe the lovemaking
does lose some of its novelty.
Maybe he admits he's threatened
by all these close friendships
I've enjoyed over the single years.
Maybe we can't even agree
on how to define the word fidelity.
Maybe, in short, after a few

bumpy months, we're both stumped
by the always-daunting challenge
of a *bona-fide* commitment,
and we say we'd better just call it quits.

But no! Let's say instead,
just for the sake of speculation,
it doesn't end that way.

Let's say this thing between us
becomes more like a treasure
we have the guts and nerve
and heart to claim. Let's say,
just for the sake of hopefulness,
we find out we like each other's
families (most of them anyway)
and agree pretty much on what to eat
and whose turn it is to find or fix it.
Maybe we introduce our friends
without any major complications.
Maybe we figure out how to merge
and manage our money too.

Let's go so far as to say
that on one dark, fearful, tearful night,
we both find ourselves giving up
priorities we thought we needed
more than we need each other.
Let's say, just for the sake of . . . love,
the two of us at last discover ourselves
right here in it, after all, and against all odds.

Reason enough, wouldn't you say,
to go to that Midtown party
I'm thinking of skipping tonight,
reason enough to reach unthinking
for one of the tempting appetizers?

1997

Romance

My life is the book I would have writ, but I could not both live and utter it.
– HENRY DAVID THOREAU

Such a plot these two are pacing.
I'm anxious for each new episode.
It recently became a love story
after various shallow, torrid scenes.

These lead characters have such a time.
Strong reasons have been raised
against their fervent hopes,
and yet their hopes are gaining.

Amor vincit omnia?
I trust it does – because it has.
The elder, waspish one
bends as once he never
could or would've done.

The younger? Well,
what can a reader make of him?
Natural as his native Brazil,
beautiful and big of heart,
wearing it out on his sleeve.

And they do say such crazy things!
I cannot live with you!
I cannot live without you.
I cannot live with you.
I cannot live without you!

And so this narrative unfolds.
I cheer for both of them –
for the thickening plot of their passion.
Haply I can wait to know
how this romance will end.

2009

Bedfellows

this little room an everywhere – JOHN DONNE

Total dark of three a. m.
makes a flesh-wide world of us,
and I want you even more now,
not for that again,
but to spoon forever here

in the sweet ambiance
of bedclothes and skin.
I want us here together
this harmonious way
as even in troubled sleep

you take the half-conscious
thrust of my calming hand
under your warm arm
around your warm breast,
easing back into our curve;

as, not even waking,
you twine your fingers
tentatively in with mine,
a sworn, wordless lovers' pact
that cannot be denied.

Beautiful, golden lover,
how viscerally I have you now,
have our sleepy tides of breathing,
the adventures of our dreams.

I swear I'll gladly surrender
a daily mind and the dubious good I do
earning space in a dissipated world,
for this warm nest of natural loving.

2009

The Broken Open Heart

The heart has got to open in a fundamental way. – LEONARD COHEN

There is a crack in everything. That's how the light gets in. – Ibid.

And must this elder heart of mine
to open, be enlightened, be so broken?

I've loved so much already:
sainted elder
in that doting maiden aunt;
decent, caring parents;
outstanding friends
(one unique one too
for over half a century now);
a wife for thirteen years;
sons grown and elsewhere now;
granddaughter, grandsons
growing away as well;
friends who once were more than friends.

Love's intense incarnations.

But not until you
gave me such a seismic shake
did I dare dream, imagine, guess
how complete, how amazing
such a quaking, such awakening could be.

Cohen has another telling line:

Every heart to love will come, but like a refugee.

2011

Old Roswell Cemetery

October 13, 2011

We will grieve not, rather find
Strength in what remains . . . – WILLIAM WORDSWORTH

Mellow autumn afternoon,
we two meander arm in arm,
strolling plot to plot
beneath old arching oaks and pines
that crown a moss-capped
most-neglected hill
of peace and solitude.

Mere yards away
an ongoing din of wheels,
brakes, sirens,
clamorings of all the living,
in all their busyness,
oblivious to this mute
memento mori.

We lament the toll of time
and vandals: a toppled obelisk;
a rusted, hanging fence;
wingless angel, all askew;
broken headstone;
words of love and loss,
less legible, fall after fall.

I tell you Shelley's sonnet:
Egyptian Ramses II,
legendary king of kings,
his massive statue ruined,
still bearing at its base
the then-proud, now pathetic taunt:

Look on my works ye mighty
and despair.

I cheerfully suggest
we *not* despair,
though all our works endure
the same demise
as all things come to pass
till even earth must die.

You readily agree, dear man:

Let's rather love the more
this life we yet may spend.

Lightning

There is a blindness in your presence,
followed by the sight of you when you are gone. – WITTER BYNNER

Piercing brightness
flashes
from deep, dark eyes.

Golden energy
trembles
through lithe, quick limbs.

You've come like shafts
of lightning
across my midnight sky

scattering all my
witty words
like startled wrens.

But look now,
my stunning lover,
how I struggle

for some
sharp metaphor
not half so shocking

as each heaven-
glimpse of you
I long to have again.

2014

Gift

Love is not as simple as getting up
on the wrong side of the bed wearing the emperor's clothes.
– BILLY COLLINS

Ainda quando estava na barriga de minha mãe, sabia que te amava.
– GILSON de ASSIS SATEL

You have broken my heart
open, like the old cocoon
I was long past needing.

You've stripped me bare
of the emperor's clothes
most saw through anyway.

Who besides you divined
the merit of this match?
How do I honor such a gift?

I can strive to emulate
the man you are,
the one you think I am.

2014

No Regrets

I thought I might not be
in crazy love with you,
so strangely unlike me,
I so unlike you.

But that thought begs a word
of explanation here:
Whatever I preferred,
no matter what I feared,

the love you grant me now,
the lessons hereby learned,
have clearly shown me how
real happiness is earned.

2017

Settlements

I wasn't going to settle,
she claimed, proud,
infatuated even,
with her fine new catch.

But who doesn't settle?
Having no choice in our birth,
we settle for being here,
long as our lives allow.

We settle from earliest days
in imperfect parental arms,
for the comfort they can offer,
until we settle for more, or less.

We settled for dates we got
including embarrassments
we thought would never end,
for friends at times unfriendly,

dull lessons, jobs – our lives,
and for folks we tolerated,
appreciated even,
for sharing theirs with us.

We settled for love,
as, when, and where it arrived
in all the tricky forms it took,
the ones we recognized.

We've settled for settling,
maybe not calling it that –
or settled for *never* settling,
for wistful solitude instead.

We'll inescapably settle
for taking our final breath

as flesh and bone will settle
into the dust of earth's dry bed.

All that said, I'll settle for you
as long as you settle with me,
if only to scratch each other's backs
before we settle for sleep.

2018

Long-term Relationship

Be wet with a decent happiness. – ROBERT CREELEY

We've ebbed and flooded,
neap tides and spring,
through storms and calms
of seasons immemorial.

We've cast up our driftwood,
welcomed it back again,
lapped our shoreline lazily,
consumed with passion

this enduring counterpoint
along our easing boundaries.
And still we live to drench
each thirsty grain of sand,

and still our vast, absorbent
shore wants every wave
for all its ineffable,
salty wetness.

2018

Good Husbandry

A few pocketed seeds
from a discarded pod somewhere
he saves for later sowing.

A pinched-off branch
from a wayside bush
along our evening walk
puts down its small
white roots in water
at the kitchen window now,
almost ready, he says,
to be set out in good, rich dirt,
its vegetation tended.

Even the dark-brown egg
inside an avocado
we shared ten years ago
is now becoming,
if you can believe,
a broad-leafed, eight-foot tree.

His state of mind
recalls the ancient Greek
a philosophical friend of mine
explained to me just recently:
a *eudaemonia*.

It equals *happiness* for sure,
if you see this man
playing out his garden passion –
but not just that exactly.
It's more like *flourishing*,
my friend translated,
and do we evermore
get countless flowers here.
all in their own good time.

The two great green gardenias
hid from too much noon heat
beneath the flowering peaches
and pruned by him last summer
shoot again from pale bullets
every spring white blooms
that lull a passer-by
into near-hypnosis, caught
in the waft of their aroma.

It's a *good daemonic*:
We watch him working,
happy demon,
those roots and shoots
and leaves and buds
and finally flowers.

Before its dark allusion,
demon did once mean
a *deity* or *genius*,
like the one my hero Socrates
reportedly had –
a guardian that never told him
what *to* do,
but stopped him in his steps
if ever he was about to do
anything he shouldn't.

This husband of mine
has just that inspiration
as he manages his happy province
around the homeplace,
season succeeding season.

Desiccated bulbs tossed aside
from a lost spray of blooms
for our Aurora's last birthday
became stargazers again
in the front yard this spring.

Love takes off the masks . . .

A redolent half-dozen
rendered the walk to the mailbox
almost overwhelming
every day for days.

That avocado plant
is now a tall, proud topiary,
limbs corded up
into a flourishing green menorah.

So many compassionate ways
he has to work and play,
and so much flourishing here,
night and day.

2020

Departure

One of us must be the last
left here to say goodbye

in farewell of bereavement,
words unheard and no reply.

I know this will sound selfish,
but it should be you, not I.

2020

They Call It Falling

epithalamium for Jay Pee and Randall, joined in flight

Let there be spaces in your togetherness. – KAHLIL GIBRAN

Whether it's a slippery slope
down to some bedeviled den
of cauldron troubles
or a high crag crested,
vistas to far horizons,
you twin climbers prep
to spread fledged wings,
take your dauntless flight,
soar like a happy pair
of gleaming eagles.

Love! Such a simple word
means flying, falling,
means risks and dangers,
means dreams gleaned.

In the Senoi tribe
of faraway Malaysia,
an elder asks all ages
seated around the breakfast fire
for last night's dreams.

A child reports a falling dream –
the fear, the cold,
the sweaty relief on waking.

Father tells him, *Fly next time.*
Fly to where that dream may take you.
And reliably they do, no longer falling.

Afterwards he asks them,
What did you learn
in that numinous realm
your spirit took you to?

*What wisdom did you gain
to give us now?*

From mouths of babies
and brave lovers
such priceless lessons come.

May you two happy fliers
soar and land back faithfully.
Show us how it's done,
and tell us what you learn.

And when you fall,
as all the daring do,
let it be as your feet fall,
stepping forward freely
along your chosen pathway,
arm on shoulder,
arm round waist.

Let yours be fairest
flying, falling weather.
Rise and fall in love
over and over again together.

Let your love thrive
as the moon thrives,
forever flying, falling,
neither too far nor near,
but safe in the embrace
of a doting earth.

2019

Don't Stop Kissing!

for all fifty lost in Orlando, June 12, 2016

gaiety transfiguring all that dread – WILLIAM BUTLER YEATS

Poor, benighted Omar
saw two young men kiss
which evidently steeled
in him some dark resolve
to rage against such love,
love choked within himself,
a chafing grain of sand
in one sorely damaged oyster
that could not make a pearl.

Don't leave him out!
Count him now
foremost among the lost,
self-victimized before
he struck his victims.

And then last night's
memorial event:

Don't Stop Kissing!

What a trove of talent.
Such stricken, thriving love.
such heartfelt keening
over wracking grief,
so many freed-up tears,
such *anger, rage*!

And finally our modicum
of mutual consolation.

A poet shared the first few
of grief's excruciating stages
he still struggles to complete,

turning horror into beauty,
a lifelong task for anyone.

A young Latina,
choked with tears
repeatedly wiped away
with a hem of her sweater,
highlighted a wrenching
account of her gay friend,
his own suffering.

Mariana of Puerto Rico
witnessed to us bravely
that almost all the lost
hailed from the island.

A talented actor –
not in an act last night –
commanded the stage
without note or script
to recall her first
and every other kiss
she ever savored,
including the ones
she trusts she will,
inspiring us,
as an old song counsels,
Let's keep dancing!

The poet's poet,
good friend Franklin,
seasoned, not desensitized
from ministering to decades
of senseless dying,
got up one more time
to read an old one,
truer than ever tonight:
You cannot kill us.

Love takes off the masks . . .

And so much more
communal suffering
through the terror.

We worked and work
to wake again
and then again
from nightmares
grim as this one.

So much determination
to not stop speaking,
dancing, kissing, loving –
as if we ever would.

2016

*Gladly would he learn,
and gladly teach.*

– GEOFFREY CHAUCER

Oral Book Reports

We all had to give them.
Some trembled at the task.
I recall one skinny kid,
his face blanched in fear
as unforgiving sunrays
beat down on him
in front of God and the rest of us
one school-day morning.
We watched in fascination
as he dashed from class
to be sick in the boys' room
while others dreaded their turns.

Not me though.
Ham that I was and am,
I squelched the nervousness
of anticipation and got up there
to tell all about my book,
one I'd actually loved reading.

Some probably sneered
at such an obedient teacher's pet.

Miss Whoever smiled
approvingly though
from behind her oak desk
with the little silver bell
she'd *ding-ding-ding*
to quiet us down when needed.

Books on her approved list
told of countless lives,
none of which we'd yet lived,
imagined lives few of us
would ever live:
pirate escapades
we once played out,

clueless how brutal and filthy
such an existence was and is;
flawless friendships
we'd be lucky ever to find;
sci-fi fantasies that helped turn
some kids into engineers.

Youth romances made us
think such miracles
would come our way
without breaking
our hearts wide open.

Most of us dutifully heeded
the teacher's warning
not to give away too much.
(Some couldn't anyway,
not having read that far.)

If you want to see how it ends,
I advise you to read the book,
we'd tell our classmates,
all of us straight-faced.
I never saw anyone
eagerly jot down a title
to go check out and read
from our musty school library.

And as for living out the narratives
of our own stranger-than-fiction lives,
we all kept right on reading
and reporting on them
in earnest for decades
to the mixed reviews of others,
managing not to panic,
careful not to reveal
or even guess our endings.

2015

Penmanship

What I might be I learned to tell in eyes which loved me.
– EDGAR BOWERS

Three teachers in a lifetime is the very best of luck.
– JOHN STEINBECK

You'll no longer see that subject
in any curriculum I know of.

But long live the rare legacy
of Mrs. Katherine Hood,
stocky, red-head emissary
from a world of learning adventure
to our dusty little pulp-wood town –
my fifth-grade teacher, mentor, friend.

Offhandedly one day
she offered me a choice,
noting I was free to make it on my own:
Would you like to practice writing better?

I agreed, teacher-pleaser
I usually was back then,
and she surprised me, just me,
with a penmanship booklet,
guide out of which, on lined tablet,
I aped in studious, deliberate cursive,
bent over my kid-sized desk,
tongue poked out to the side,
alone in a crowded classroom,
learning in my personal space and pace
how to turn my chicken scratching
into those flowing, elegant
letters and phrases.

I didn't stick with the project long.
She never raised the subject again either –
except to mention that I'd improved.

I still felt I'd failed somehow,
meant to do a better, thorough job.
But that personal attention,
let's just say it – *love,*
impressed two telling points
on pre-teen me back then:
I was already the captain of my fate,
and by the way, my writing should
and could become more legible.

Or, the twig was bent before,
back when I first saw my sainted
aunt's well-rounded penmanship,
nicer even than lines in that book,
more deliberate, somehow more virile.
I did my best to imitate her elder craft
in all the dutifully penned letters
she and I exchanged in our years apart.

Now I scribble rarely, quickly.
Time has brought a tremble to my pen.
Carting down the grocery aisle
I squint to read the item
I scratched on my list a day ago.
I sign my name now
as if I were someone famous.

Think how many elders
must have once lamented
lost calligraphic skills,
illuminated back in Darker Ages,
not to mention even older
hieroglyphic lore –
however fine and careful
their own penmanship
may well have been.

2020

Formless Education

High school science led me to a conclusion:
Essentially, we and every other thing
are more-or-less varying concentrations of molecules.
I saw how atom drawings in my textbooks
looked remarkably like little solar systems.

I could almost see invisible people living on electrons
swirling with others around a luminescent nucleus –
in my own glow-in-the-dark watch dial maybe –
except that I've more recently found out
electrons aren't at all so localized or earth-like.

Now I hear it's even stranger than I thought.
As Sir James Jeans once mystically observed,
*The universe is looking less like a great machine
and more and more like a great thought –*
quite enough to stymie all my notions.

Photons being neither-here-nor-there,
however carefully we work to look
for them, should make us question further
any ordinary four-dimensional view
of what we choose to call our real, familiar world.

Meanwhile here I am still, or seem to be
at least, seated at a home computer desk
eyeing a monitor critically as it adds, letter
by letter, words and even poems made possible,
I gather, by those same inscrutable particles.

2016

Donors

Westwood High School

Black man,
White man,
each on a bed.

White man,
Black man,
blood deep red.

197_

School

Adolescents stream
along wide corridors,
round-eyed and flippant.

Frenzied small-fry
dart through the current
amid bright swerving
of muscle and tail

pursued by a sharp-toothed
bell that propels them
in doorways

into our classrooms,
packed in tens.

1978

Why I Hope You've Been Taking Notes

For English 607, Spring 1973

It's been a mysterious thing, you know –
because I never knew (not really)
what I had that you should use,
and you never knew what I might offer,
so you couldn't possibly have known for sure
what to listen to or what to doze through,
and I could never be sure what to review
for the upcoming test (for life's test),
so I had to listen to my heart – and to you.

Some of what I shared came marching forth
disguised in the sable robes of academia,
and some of it just slipped right out
like a naked two-year-old escaping a dreaded bath.

But as we plunged through such complexities,
I hope you took some kind of legible notes,
because we don't know for sure how profound
a thing we may have been involved in here anyway,
and because some of us, someday, are sure
to need to remember some of these things,
and because I expect to continue to need
to wrestle with all these same absurdities,
perhaps with some of you again eventually,

because it's a small world in ways you never dreamed,
and it's a large world in ways I never dreamed,
and because I've loved you as none of us ever dreamed,
and because the beauty of this whole business
of being alive is a mystery which only together
we can continue daring to dream.

Testing Instructions

There is a crack, a crack in everything. That's how the light gets in.
– LEONARD COHEN

You've got to take it today, kid,
whether you like it or not, got to take it today.
The purpose isn't to prepare you for life;
this *is* life, and if it's to be taken at all, today's the day.

And you're what you have to take it with, kid.
Here's your simple assignment:
Create for yourself the light of the sun again.
Let there be light now from in and out of you
in a strange new unpredictable illumination,
in a never-before-dreamed-of elucidation.

You haven't a minute to review for this test
because there's only the one view, anyway.
It's before you now, and it *is* the test.

But can you remember what you knew
before you walked into this stark hall,
took your sharpened, electronically sensitive pencils,
and sat down insensitively to take it?
That's the crucial part of the answer, isn't it now?

You won't remember,
unless you boldly drop your classroom tools,
forget time and place, end all thought of trying.
Then you'll glimpse again what it was like outdoors
in the real light of the real sun created then by Father's wisdom
for a garden filled with Mother's roses swaying
in domesticated beds with winding paths defining them.

Look for it now, kid, look for it now,
that garden of rosebuds dime-a-dozen,
where you danced a dance you've since forgotten.
This is the challenge pending now before you.

Was it *Chase me till I catch you in the dusk*,
while fireflies rise like winking constellations,
luring us into dreamy midsummer darkness
where the light fails and Puck runs wild,
till finally no one calls us in because we're too old now,
and worlds away from that quaint, wondrous life?

So now we've wandered here
into the artificial bright fluorescence
where the graphite number-twos swish meticulously,
marking plausible electronic spots,
omitting responses in cases of utter doubt,
on a non-spindled, non-mutilated, testing form
which is now timed, machine-gradable, and multiple-choice,
two possibilities of which are, *All of the above*, and *None*.

But listen to me, kid, listen with me:
Keep a loving lookout
for that sunny garden where the crimson roses grow.
It's nothing less than the lost land of paradise
for which we all are wondering, know it or not.

And for future reference, kid, believe me,
the best of the test is after the answer sheet is marked
and the scratch paper's dutifully surrendered,
after you've wanly anticipated an acceptable grade
in the mail on a print-out from heaven
which, though it's scored by an accurate scanning light,
is only a shade of the light that's capable
of shining its way right in and out of you.

Meanwhile, today, enjoy your break.
Use it to ponder that glimpse of the dance in the garden.
Remember that glimpse of the garden, kid.
It isn't yet that far away.

1974

Goodbye,

rainbow-girl
of legion
metaphors
in arching
kodachromes,
watcher
of vermilion
sunrise,
stroller in
the small
grey rain
(over cobble-
stones in
Tango Lane),
rider of the
lime-green
sea waves,
rider high
on wild,
winged horses
tossing
frothy
moonlit manes
(cousins of
your early-
morning
unicorn),
singer of
slender bird-
flute
phrasings,
dreamer,
daring toucher
of passion-reds
and frozen
blues and
countless
other bright
surprises
sent out in
slim, divine
disguises.
Indeed, you are
no earthling!
(See, I've
learned a
lot from you!)
But I'll have
other lovely
students.
Perhaps,
(perhaps)
another
vernal poet
evocative
of you
to speak our
language too.
So go on,
have your level
head, make
your own
weaving
way now.
Go on seeing,
gathering up
the glinting
scatters
of your fine
prismatic name.
But once
upon a
now-and-then
(no matter
when)
send me back
another lyric
line or two.
For there's an
old cliché
that got that
way by being
true:
Never (never)
will there be
another you.

1974

Was Melville Also Gay?

                1.

As an English teacher (closeted myself)
standing before a frisky class of teens,
I heard the comment on occasion,
always a boy who blurted it out
in negative fascination: *That's so gay!*
Something in the lesson struck him
as dangerously, grossly homoerotic –
Ishmael and Queequeg bedded together
or even two females embracing.

The boy's adolescent sense of self,
ramrod straight (and especially if not),
required him to distance himself
or at least appear to claim some space
from what he felt was just too queer
to him to let go by without a protest.

I'd always ask, as if I didn't know,
Now what's that supposed to mean?

Oh, never mind, Mr. P, he'd say
and duck his naive head,
wishing he hadn't triggered
my stock response, given as always
for all the good it may have done:

Is gay supposed to be a bad thing?
It's not an illness or a choice, you know.

And then I might go on to add
that separate beds were hard to get
in nineteenth-century Massachusetts,
leaving unmentioned that Melville,
so I'd read, had been a closet case like me.

I always thought of that statistical one
in every ten kids sitting in the room
needing desperately to know
that someone they respected
thought being gay was perfectly OK.

          2.

One early morning, well before first bell,
Bill,* himself a striking Billy Budd,
dropped by as he sometimes liked to do
to say hello – and sometimes ask for a hug,
in the good old days before touching
a student in any manner at all was forbidden.

This time though, he teared up
in the safety of that office space
and told me, reddened eyes aglisten,
a secret burden of his youth: rape
when he was 12, by another boy, 16.

No healer I, but loving him
more than he would ever come to know,
I tendered my sincere condolence,
asked if the pain had been physical
besides being emotional, as I could see.

He said he'd bled from that abuse.

It was, I agreed, a vicious insult,
but I asked if a part of his suffering
was a haunting thought that two males
having sex at all was wrong.

He said *No* (maybe only guessing
the answer I hoped he'd give),
it wasn't because it was gay,
but just the fact it was forced on him,
he readily explained.

3.

When I was a college sophomore,
before I'd heard about Herman,
or even about myself in fact,
I had a term paper to do, but couldn't decide
between researching Whitman's *Leaves of Grass*
or Melville's *Moby Dick.*

Dr. Davis, a gruff but congenial sort,
advised me as we strolled
from his world lit class one day,

*Do Melville. That's more like
something that ought to interest you.*

I didn't ask and now will never know
why he thought it best to steer me out to sea
among those lusty ship-board sailors,
far from Whitman's lusty city.

2012

*Not his actual name.

For Marc*

Sunlit youth, he lounges easily
atop a dune beside me, sugary sand
partway up his arms and shins,
chatting breezily of this and that,
squinting out across a sparkling bay,
as if to glimpse a life unknown to him.

So innocent, so unaware –
so handsome too, this adolescent boy.
Both of us with downcast eyes,
I sift warm sand oh-so-suavely
from an hour-glass of fist, silently
admiring him more than he could know.

1986

*Marc graduated secondary school in Germany at age eighteen but joined a group of exchange students who visited our school that year. I took all of them, along with a number of our students, for a weekend backpacking trip on St. Joseph's Peninsula in Florida. Marc referred to me as his "American father" that he felt more comfortable with than he did with his host parents. Our friendship that year meant at least as much to me as it did to him.

Youth Counselor

One comes to tell him
how she loathes her parents,
wishes them dead in hell
and herself back in Paris
with Anton again.

Another slouches mutely in the chair.
He's sick and tired of living
with an alcoholic father
ever since the divorce turned Mom
into a whacked-out pseudo-psychic
who can't let his teen energy near her aura.

The well-groomed, overly polite one
makes a formal appointment,
finally breaks down and sobs today,
says he broods on jumping
off a certain expressway bridge.

Then comes a boy of just eighteen
frustrated in love (or lust) with a boy fifteen
in his Sunday school class.
Reluctantly, he manages to see
what a risky bind he's in.

Another wants to date the fellow
who kisses her in the back room
at the doughnut shop,
keeps telling her how pretty she is.
She'd rather not discuss
his wife and baby daughter.

The last one admires him with big doe eyes,
wants an after-school appointment next time,
wants to help him with his reticence
against her blameless devotion,
wants their friendship to be perfect.

He listens long and gingerly,
encouraging, coaching as he can,
then heads on home
to bills and a hungry cat.

He turns the phone off
and soaks away referred pain
of adolescent sufferings
in a restorative hot bath,
browsing last month's copy
of *Psychology Today*.

198_

Therapeutic Observations

a found poem*

You're an intensity junkie.
You do have a knack for tearing up the scenery.
We don't have to pathologize that.
Just turn down the volume and look at the picture.
What vows have you taken?

Most of therapy is helping people defend themselves.
Here's a mantra for you: Limit the *bon mots* and just *be dull*.
Be sparing of quoting Socrates to people.
Life is not a proving ground.
You have perfectionistic tendencies.
Do you feel you're good enough yet?

Avoid taking inventory on people who haven't requested it.
Filter the thoughts you share.

You get more when you tell the truth.
What do you want, what do you need, and what's best for you?
Are you getting enough from life?

Strong stimulants are a slippery slope for us all.
It's good to go without them at times.

We all give away our power when we get upset.
You might not always get the wise award.
Your power comes from calm, kind thought and action.

Is it okay to have a bad day?
Don't pour gasoline on the fire.
Don't shit in the nest.
Keep the communication when the heat is on.
Don't be your partner's teacher.

You're learning to deal with all kinds of people.
Some of them just want a stand-up cardboard you.

Don't keep going to a dry well for water.
Resist the urge to contend with a tar baby.
You may be dealing with a borderline personality or two.
Sometimes, don't open your heart, just maintain good behavior.
Sometimes, just sit back and watch the top spin.
Consequences are not punishments.
You do this, you get this; you do that, you get that.

Love may never die, but it can become nostalgia.
A long-term love-life requires due diligence.
There's nothing like strange.
You two appear to have a viable relationship.
You get to have that, you know.

You sure know how to scare him.
I love my partner more every day.
Yesterday I hung up on him.

You're ambitious.
You have a lot of curiosity.
You make good use of your time here.
I'm glad things are going well for you.
Keep up the good work.

2016

*These were all memorable comments and questions from my skilled life coach, made on different occasions and collected over a period of decades. I chuckle when I think how often I still like to mention Socrates.

Memento Mori

because to be here is so much – RANIER MARIA RILKE

Shaken at four a. m.
from the old nightmare:
me striving for attention and respect
from a class of thoughtless teens.

I did well back then, with modest toil
and ample satisfactions, though exceptions
do loom cloudy over my nostalgia:
the chaos in my class on chaos theory,

the day I intoned from up on my dais
after being nagged beyond my patience
a student's answer on a test was simply *wrong!*
Her curt comeback? *No kidding!*

The boy who truly believed
I'd claimed *all* Christians are hypocrites,
the one who shot a withering glare
and spit at me, *We are* not *brothers!*

Sometimes I get a glad surprise.
A thoughtful former student, up in years now,
writes that I gave her a love for poems.
A man recalls what my praise had meant.

They make it sunshine clear again:
it was a marvelous career,
on balance so rewarding, humbling,
fulfilling far beyond my pride.

So why this damning dream again?
Finally I may have a pre-dawn answer,
after our mountain outing yesterday
through autumn-gilded woods

past cascades gushing their hearts out
with never a care for anyone's opinion,
an easy trek for the younger guys,
more of a trial for these old shanks.

Is it obsolescence – death – I fear
despite my sunny smiles and pastimes?
And why should anyone need to be
a retired teacher on a hike, or dreaming,

instead of any living, loving one of us,
on any daunting path to truth, joy, beauty,
to suffer this way (in our sleep at least)
such an almost never-ending dread?

2018

Incident

Humility is endless. – T. S. ELIOT

Once, expounding
in my English-teacher way
to an indulgent friend,
There are *no accidents!*
an idea I probably gleaned
from some old heresy I'd read,

the over-reaching sweep
of my glib arm and hand
sent a hapless glass of wine
air-borne, skidding to the floor,
gushing purple fingers of fate
across the beige carpet.

We laughed at the irony,
and I felt duly chastened
by whatever powers be.
I did *not* want the wine to spill,
the rug to stain – eager only
to make my cavalier claim.

Of course I hadn't planned
that demonstration.
No, the unforeseen served well
to contradict my naive notions,
which is all they ever are
vis a vis the All we never know.

2011

Vacation

This morning before I woke
with that familiar relief
(and a stuffy nose from dry heat),
I'd been busily frustrated
cleaning out my teacher space
for vacation, actually for retirement.

All the dog-eared, marked-up
books I'd shelved to bolster
the lore I disseminated,
if not perpetrated,
onto green minds and even
hearts of teens assigned to me.

All the care-worn stuff of pedagogy –
but why that stash of twisted toys,
cordless lamps, the useless
hardware cached away,
boxes full of nameless things,
the games with missing pieces?

What should I entrust to dutiful
custodians who'll serve on
now that I'm gone, what to toss
on a campus dump, and who
will follow me to use, perhaps,
old materials I think to leave her?

And how do I heft the rest all down
the stairwells of a school
estranged now, how to pack
a trove of cherished souvenirs
into a space, now so constrained,
of a vehicle that will get me home somehow.

And where do I drive off to now,
what awaits my fresh arrival,

and why review, decades after
the actual deed, and in this wistful dream,
departure made with no ado – unless
to foretell yet another clearing out?

2020

This Garden

Those who know do not speak, and talkers never know. – Tao Te Ching

*I know you are reading this poem listening for something, torn
between bitterness and hope,
turning back once again to the task you cannot refuse.* – ADRIENNE RICH

This deadliest year in American history,
I simply need to be –
in some exquisitely appointed garden,
like ones I've celebrated in before
or maybe ones I've seen in movies,
dreamed of several times,
waking happily wet-eyed.
I suspect you know this refuge.

Mine's a breathing space
the brave hero (or in my case
the ordinary guy like me)
retreats into for needed restoration
before he faces back to doing battle
with all the hydra-headed threats
to health and happiness,
truth and decency,
including those that lurk within him.

Maybe it's a padlocked garden.
Paradise is lost. Kingdom has not come
and isn't gainable again for the duration.

Maybe it's one of those fantasy tales
on a far-flung planet in a sci-fi galaxy,
one like my sheltering partner
encourages me to enjoy with him.

But I recognize this space, I do,
all now serene and placid.
Breathless as we may have been,
our breath resumes – slow and easy.

All within this holy fold
is lovely order, perfect stillness.
Even the randomly situated rocks
in this tended geometric courtyard
are content – just being dry old stones,
the way I sometimes see myself – forged,
washed, and tumbled for eons in the river,
smooth and unassuming, intact for now.

I'll rise as my hoped-for host arrives
to greet me. We'll bow, make *Namaste*.
He'll be robed and shorn – and merry!

Think of the smile of Thich Nhat Hanh
or the Dalai Lama's curious grin
curling even now above my keyboard
as if to say, *All's well and shall be well.*

What a welcome apparition!
Such modesty of emptiness, whole
and hollow, silver flute awaiting wind.

It could be dear old wizened Yoda
smiling, radiating all and nothing,
swaying his unassuming head
as he intones, *We do not try.*
We simply do or we do not do.
I'd then be just as energized.

Tea is brought without a sound
(much as I might think a little Sake
would have soothed me quicker).

I confess I've never celebrated
such a salving ritual as this one,
but it's a state of mind we sorely want
as pestilence keeps right on killing,
driving us to shelter in our fear.

So tell me, fellow farer, if you will
muster all your marshaled wit and wisdom,
what our imagined sage will say (if anything)
as we savor contemplative sips of tea
before we go back out to suffer more
our simple task and duty.

2020

Observation

There are some things which cannot be learned quickly, and time, which is all we have, must be paid heavily for their acquiring. They are the very simplest things. – ERNEST HEMINGWAY

Those very simplest things
take long to comprehend because
evidently our "common sense"
(neither common nor a sense)
imagines broad complexities
that rise like grey fog banks
creating clouds of confusion –
while truth, like misplaced
reading glasses, sits quietly
atop an absent-minded head.

197_

One long cry from the heart of the artist: Give me the chance to do my very best.

– *BABETTE, IN THE FILM,* BABETTE'S FEAST

Found Art

We guess how it began:

a rainy winter night outside,
a flickering fire,
a tell-tale bulge on the cave wall
the size of a prized
and sought-out creature,
lacking only head,
legs, horns, and tail,

needing only a tribal teller
to scribe such features
with a charred fire-stick
to animate a vital heritage
for the sheltered clan.

When did some elder
hold up a driftwood limb
curved like a goose
and honk to the giggles
in a gaggle of kids?

Last summer at the beach?
Or maybe that little joke
eased the pain and tedium
of a treacherous migration
some millennia long gone.

Just so, my fellow and I,
on our sunlit ramble
through Roswell woods,
spot an ice-white quartz stone
in the shape of a heart,
or a weathered gnarl
just like a human face:

Look, two eyes here,
a twisted nose below!

We pocket them
and take them home
to keep on patio or mantle.

What nature never needs to mean
we clothe in meanings.

2012

Little Ode

Tell us why
we love you so,
Vincent
van Gogh.

Because

(I have him say)

*out of that black gloom
no one ever fathoms,
doggedly I daubed
a multicolored cosmos
of rippling leaves
and rolling fields,
anguished sunflowers,
furrowed faces,
a twirling* t'ai chi chuan
*of midnight sky,
with moon, stars –
a small blue room. . . .*

Because

*brushing my way
through ten crazed years,
I transfigured
so much torment,
leaving you these signs.*

1985

Across the Street & into the Hemingway House

For Rob at the Lighthouse Court
for telling me about your father's sweet goodbye

All the best ones, when you thought it over, were gay. It was much better to be gay and it was a sign of something too . . . like having immortality while you were still alive. — ERNEST HEMINGWAY

Not at all my favorite author,
despite the way that quote can now be read,
but the steady tropical drizzle today
and the place situated just directly across
from this most un-Hemingwayesque guest house,
I decide to endure the other tourists and have a look.

And well worth it too, if only to see
how someone with fame and wealth would live.

Inside the high brick wall, a comfortable hacienda
in the now-faded style of the thirties,
though a chandelier was missing,
and I knew not all that stuff was ever his.
Besides, what may have been
looked so much like cheap copies today
I was slow to appreciate its value.
And who did the place up anyway, the wife?
No pansy he, wouldn't the bright floral draperies
have been hers to order?

I could just about hear the old bull
raging at the insipid lot of us,
throwing us out on our ears.

Didn't he commit suicide? someone muttered.

I saw their spacious upstairs bedroom,
huge bed, headboard a Spanish gate,
tall French doors onto the surrounding balcony,

doors our guide said they never curtained,
being far enough from the street
(or maybe Ernest wanted anyone
who happened to look close enough to see
how ramrod straight he really was).

In the crowded silence of the room
I could imagine us all thinking,
So this is where they made love.
We even gawked shamelessly,
into the quaint adjoining bathroom.

Poor, macho, one-true-sentence American hero
with all your props – strung-up marlin on the wall,
heads of wild beasts – but your own head
blown away in Idaho years ago.

Drank a helluva lot, I think, someone volunteered.

And then the kindly old guide's comment
on manic depression, ranking you, Ernest, up
(and down) with the likes of Napoleon and Churchill,
correlating the ailment with gifted intellects,
a disease I don't have to worry about,
he chuckled modestly.

Then I slipped away from the tour
to visit your carriage house,
the whole top floor one clean, well-lighted room
where you did so much honest, decent work.

Alone in the emptiness only an artist knows,
you once shuffled, as I see your ghost now,
among your books and writing tools.

Troubled genius,
repressed, homophobic, finally paranoid man –
all toughness and tight-lipped scorn.

Once, drunk, you wrecked that Key West bar
like a frat boy on a rampage,
carrying a ripped-off urinal home –
a souvenir of what exactly, Ernest?

I found that sentence of yours
in a book of someone else's poems.
Not that it's true
or even means what I want it to,
but much as it might have annoyed you,
I love you for even writing it.

It's almost like hearing my own long-lost Papa
finally tell me it's all OK.

1996

Door of the Heart

What fine works, what
testimonies are displayed here:
paintings, bas-reliefs.

Guests in a bright white gallery
test the snacks and sip Chablis.

Critically we scan
the efforts of a man
whose labor is devotion.

Most of us stare rapt
at our favorite,
large as life itself,
title on a telling card:

Door of the Heart.

Rainbows of oils glisten
over tooled woodwork
worthy of a portal
opening into paradise.

Sensual, beckoning, this
gateway to all redemption
and reward –

yet no hint of handle or knob!

Asked about the omission
when he strolls over,
our silver-haired artist
has a ready reply.

He's heard this question before.
He lives out his self-encouraged days
its simple-but-not-easy answer.

One long cry from the heart of the artist: . . .

With hand outstretched
in a casual gesture
toward his door, he smiles
betraying a hint of hesitation,
but with a teasing twinkle too:

*Come on, I'm sure you know
the door of the heart
always opens from inside.*

2011

Blockbuster Has Closed Its Doors

The magazine article lamented, and I can readily agree
that something else we loved has vanished from our lives.
No more trips to scan the racks of movie choices,
no more blurbs to read on glossy jackets, no pricey snacks
to snatch on impulse, waiting in the check-out line.

I know I'm telling my age when I ask, but what about
the *Late Show* we stayed up to see and dozed off during,
until the station, one of three, woke us with its sign-off,
flag flapping in black-and-white from a bug-eyed tube
shielded during the day by varnished cabinet doors?

And how about the drive-in, now a junkyard outside town,
where on a Saturday evening Dad steered the family car
onto a little berm at just the angle to face a wall of screen?
He'd hook the heavy steel speaker with knob for volume
onto his door, then warn us kids in back, *Settle down*.

Who remembers this: The first city cinemas had to hire
piano players to keep pace with the flickering scenes.
Placards of flowery script were briefly flashed for dialogue,
but soon a top-billed Hollywood diva was out of a job
when talkies required voices with no Brooklyn twang.

Before then, who can prove Parisians dropped their popcorn
and fled the locomotive charging onto their upholstered seats?
We find it odd to hear Athenians stood – naked, unashamed –
on an amphitheater stage where the drama involved killing –
but kept it hidden behind the scenes, shielding cultured eyes.

2013

Montage

It always rains relentlessly
as we witness another grim dilemma
tourists never catch with cameras:

takes of a driven adolescent
so gaunt and miserable we wonder
how the actor won that role.

He grows more appealing though,
scene by scene, turning his thin coat collar
against the wretched weather,

dragging forlornly on a damp *Gauloise*
all the while dogging his Juliet
finally up to a shabby garret

where she clutches him briefly at best
before vanishing like a changeling
off to the lavishly sunlit south,

to someone's impenetrable villa
where the fellow we've come to care for
can't follow. But he plods on somehow,

and we remain in the shadows, stymied too,
while matter-of-fact credits float upward
over the grieving landscape.

1982

The Bigger They Are

Michelangelo's David *sculpture at risk, experts say.–* L. A. TIMES

True, taste is inarguable,
but my fine old friend Bob
has wondered more than once,

Why does everyone think of that David
when they hear the name –
and not Donatello's?

Maybe it's because
the great white marble one
is so overwhelmingly macho
while the little brown fellow
is practically a girl, albeit bronze,
yet hardly brazen.

She looks as if she'd just left off
scrubbing scullery pots,
set a bowl atop her ringlets,
held a broom to be the sword
that pared barbaric head from massive trunk –
her hand on a cocked hip, mincing,
with a cabbage under foot,
amusing fellow kitchen drudges –

not glaring, brow furrowed with intent,
sling cocked for slaying
a living, lowering giant.

(Or so I might have claimed
just to see again my friend feign
wide-eyed horror, clutch his breast.)

Although that grander *David*
stands defiantly to hold the field,
and though he has no feet of clay,

One long cry from the heart of the artist: . . .

his existential flaw, they say,
is the crazing
mineral in his ankle,

his actual Achilles heel,

the dangerous stone,
still bearing his weight,
that in a quake one day
might bring him down.

2016

Bound to Be Read Books Is Closing.

(What's left is now half-priced.)

In this digitized age
of high-tech and bottom lines,
fewer books are bound at all,
produced by techno-magic,
consumed instead
by *Nook* or *Kindle*.

I haven't flipped that switch.
I still want the smell of paper,
my personal store-bought
pages I can dog-ear as I please,
lines underlined in pen or pencil;
still want to flip back to see years later
what's marked by hand, not finger-swiped
along a touchpad screen.

I like to see what moved me when,
what question mark or star,
what X of disagreement,
exclamation point,
or simple check of understanding
still may mark a margin;
what my passing comment was
or what I quoted there,
and may still credit now.

I like the musty smell
of little bookstores too,
soft lights and shadows
in sequestered stacks,
the physical and visible
bound-up bounty
of all that anyone ever
tried to say and share –
candy stores of the mind.

And so I went once more,
bought up a trove
of local poets who, like me,
would hope a curious reader
might someday prize
the time and trouble taken
to try new ways of seeing.

On more than one occasion
I stood up in this one,
cast my eager lines
to hook a willing audience.
It's closest to my wordsmith heart
since *Outwrite Books* is gone
with its glittery fascinations,
friends and celebrations,
jars of aromatic tea.

Now this one too
unhelped if not undone
by an Amazon phenomenon,
or the brighter barns of "nobler" deals
that sometimes lure me in.

I know, the pace
of progress presses on.
I step out with it too,
but slightly toward the rear,
glancing back a little wistfully
at favorite well-stocked spaces
I was privileged to plunder.

2015

Instrumental

I won't be sorry
to have you here,
compact cellphone,
trusty companion
weighting my pocket.

You've liberated me so often
from my flesh-bound cell
out to a world of friends,
family, fact, fiction, and fun.

And you do it so reliably,
I might even say it's mystical
to a mind like mine, ignorant
of these ever-new technologies.

Preferring you, though, to a friend
leaning across a dinner table
to whisper intimacies
to my face downturned,

or slighting now this graceful
harpist thrilling us here
with lilting strands of melody
in a hushed *sangha** tonight
would be rude and wrong.

But still I slip you out,
lift you up eye-level briefly,
(flash feature tapped discreetly off)

to catch a memorable image
from my viewpoint back here
of that lady, strumming trance-like,
harp hugged and fingered fondly

alongside an affable clarinetist
whose rustic tunes
and cakewalk syncopations
complete the harmonies.

I would no more slight you,
small as you are,
mysterious package
of endless options,
than I'd scorn this eye,
scouring endlessly
against all odds
to see things clearly –

or even my straining ear
that brings such healing,
musical atonements deep
into the hungry heart of me.

2018

*sangha *[Skt.]* – *a community of Buddhists, an assembly*

Dark Time

In the dark times
Will there also be singing?
Yes, there will also be singing
About the dark times. – BERTOLT BRECHT

Dark is what brings out your light.
– ROBERT FROST, *"Take Something Like a Star"*

Star that you are, Leonard Cohen,
you told us ominously enough

You want it darker,

title of your final, muffled farewell album
before they moved you
to that tower down the track
where you could hear Hank Williams
coughing all night long.

We blow out the light.

You tell us there, darkly enough,
not only what's before us all,
but what the last election wrought*
so that now I hear you better
this cold, grey morning.

I found you first by chance
as I was mourning a godmother gone.

You challenged my misery:

Why do you stand at the window
abandoned to beauty and scorn?
Climb on your tears and be silent
like the rose on its ladder of thorn.

One long cry from the heart of the artist: . . .

You showed me, showed us all,
the dark from the start,
taught us we wanted to see it,
needed to, whether or no.

You sang that happy, hapless, cracked,
and ultimate condition of everyone
that breaks open to let light in.

So goodbye, old man.
I raise a glass to your life and legacy.

Cold as we are, and broken,
we still sing *Hallelujah!*
and like those birds at daybreak,
we *start again*.

2018

*Cohen died November 7, 2016, a day before Donald Trump was elected president of the United States.

Travel is fatal to prejudice, bigotry, and narrow-mindedness.

– MARK TWAIN

Vignette

An adventurous four-year-old
is trotting up the aisle
in the Kroger store.

A nervous mother shrills,
*Robbie, stop that running
right this instant!*

A big, bearded stranger
grins down at him,
Run all you want to, kid.

Robbie gives him one wild look
and goes on running.

1976

Cedar Key, 1955

Oh as I was young and easy in the mercy of his means,
  Time held me green and dying
  Though I sang in my chains like the sea. – DYLAN THOMAS

Once and only
was I golden boy in dawning sun
and was it an easy living venture
loving small and free by a summertime seaside.

It was shriek of gull in sunlight,
azure on aquamarine into the far of horizon,
all colors rising, returning, and changing
to slick olive drab slopping under a creosote dock
where I crawled down under and dawdled
and dipped into water beneath bands of shining
to spy on fleets of sleek needlefish idling on wavelets.

Wash of the sea deepened and darkened beneath me,
and still how I played in the light of my day,
gazed at wet weed that rode in on the vastness of tide
to swirl at the pilings that stood down into pitch-black,
invisible sea-ooze below.

I in my jeans and my greenness was fearful,
free but not free like the water,
wary of drowning, imagining frantic rescues
from out of that mystery deep.

So it had to be love and innocence only that carried me
along that broad dock safely back daily
past papers of fish bait rotting in sun, assaulted by insects,
all mingled with sweet, briny smells from a dockside café.

I played in that ignorant strangeness
of crab traps, salt crumbs, shells, and pelicans
under a bullying sun that pinched and reddened my neck
with a bearable afternoon pain.

And long though it was, my day was unlasting.

Right down to the sundown and sea dark
this world – green, expansive, swept by the sea wind –
was once only wide world enough for the loving of me.

197_

Viejo San Juan

Lavender, lengthening shadows of twilight,
aroma of coffee brewed, just-squeezed oranges,
blue-gray cobblestones, steps of stone,
weaving of streetways between mortared homes
with weatherworn shutters, filigreed balconies,
strings of bare light bulbs looped on the plaza,
courtyards of palm trees, twined bougainvillea,
murmuring pigeons wobbling low in their cooing,
cries of street gamins, blue-gold Madonna with child
beaming down from her plinth, chained portals of shops,
bright doorways of bars, Latin guitars strummed in unison,
cantos from bistros with outflowing banter
and tinkling of glasses like wind-driven chimes –

garish *putas* displayed along Luna Street,
languidly posed in the columned arcade
(wiser than hatless boy-sailors who stumble by).

Then an outwinding byway gone narrowly climbing in stairs
up to high city ramparts, sloping away,
a height of old battlements worn by waves.

A ribbon of shoreline unwinding its margin,
and always the circular sweep of the sea.

1965

San Juan Nocturne

Tropical night-time,
sultry air and rolling breakers.
I stand peering out to sea

taking the warm night wind
that steadies shoreward
over a moon-blanched beach.

Like a child, I'm mystified by all that is,
with all that was or may have been,
and all that will and will not be.

I hear the midnight sounds,
turnings of a city barely sleeping
curved against a black and silver sea.

I call up scenes from the past –
my hometown, Florida, Turkish beer halls,
and now the present calm of a Caribbean midnight.

I search, as if for a glimpse of light
off in the darkness out at sea,
never seeing more than me.

1966

Still Night

I have been one acquainted with the night. – ROBERT FROST

I know those who sleep at night to meet the dawn and work all
    day to end at dusk, who curb desire and pray.
They live within a normal frame of things, within the routine
    safety of deeds tradition proves, in old, hereditary
    habitude.
They plant and reap and prosper, procreate and raise their young,
    and die – to prove, as if it still were cause for doubt,
    this irony of mortal humans.

But I am one who sometimes walked the night away.
Often have I blessed the end of day and left half-hearted work,
    sought dark's pungent secrets, feared its shadows, drunk
    its solitude, believed its stark negation of the daylight.
I am one who has not wanted sleep at end of day.
I have rather cared to keep a silent watch, to peer with avid eyes
    at midnight's intricacies.
Often have I walked an unpremeditated beat, sometimes grown
    sweetly weary, benumbed in body, pacing off a
    sleeping city's stones.

I have strolled naively on unfamiliar strands of beach and
    listened vaguely to the sea admonishing the shore and
    gaped, head arched, at heaven's show of stars.
And there in that cool dark, in one swift instant, I shrugged the
    yoke of worldly things and gave free thought a holiday
    and claimed infinity, breathed eternity.
Then I knew at once the unity in all that is or has been or will
    ever be.

But always far too soon that vision failed. I saw the fading
    eastern sky, the tinge of coming day.
I focused mutely back as a round, red, sedative sun locked night
    away. I felt the darkness dying, knew it would not stay
    to consummate its siren song.

So then, deserted by the clarity of night, alone, I ached in
    weariness again.
Exhausted senses neither saw nor heard another thing now that
    turning day had come.

At last, I could at least take heart at thought of sleep and find my
    bed and close my mind to dawn and contradict in deep
    repose the westward toil of sun and humans, and dream
    it was still night.

1966

Star of Venus

One
Luquillo
afternoon,
a feminine
entity
not more
than four
came up
from the surf
breathing
common air
for the very
first time
(for all I knew)
holding up
her dripping
prize.

I asked her,
Que es esto?
(I knew
but wanted
her to say.)

She beamed
a champion grin
up at me,
exclaimed
the one
bright word,
Estrella!

And so it was.

197_

Last Liberty

It was an empty-sidewalk Sunday afternoon
in Charleston, South Carolina. Tex and I
were tucked away at the VFW, looking
like ice-cream vendors in our summer whites,
swilling down four-bit draft beers at the bar.

After enough of that gold elixir
had filtered to our brains and through us
to make the country steel guitars sound lovely,
gushing out from a rainbow jukebox
brightening the dark bar shadows,
we discovered buxom, blatantly blonde Trixie.

This is when a sailor's hat slides back on his head
and his flushed face begins to radiate
all the blushing silliness of an un-spent childhood
he thought he might skip by signing up.

Well, Trixie was all ridiculous grins herself,
and our presence undeniably accentuated the magic –
not that she was young or pretty, but we didn't mind that –
or that she was sporting a shiny new wedding band.

One of the endearing things about her Clyde
was that he enjoyed bringing her down to the club
to mess around a little with harmless swabs like us.

So Tex danced with her, and I danced with her,
and then he again, closer, whispering in her perfumed ear,
I sure would like to have you,
as he proudly reported to me right afterward.

She loved every red-hot minute, apparently,
while Clyde just slouched at the bar,
chain-smoking, coughing, downing beers,
laying out quarters for the jukebox,
watching the three of us play.

Travel is fatal to prejudice . . .

Finally, after a lot of that foolishness,
Clyde danced with her himself,
both of them wobbly on the small dance floor,
but evidently all the fiddling around
had cranked up the music in their honeymoon.

Finally Tex and I slopped our goodbyes,
hugging Clyde too without thinking,
and then found our way out into sudden Sunday twilight.

In the quiet weeds behind a roadside billboard,
we enjoyed a last, long, luxurious leak,
out of mutual eye-range, need I say,
and joked nervously about how horny we were.
I'll always wonder what Tex may have had in mind,

but I for one don't see how it could have been for Trixie,
and I don't see how we could've done much about it that night,
no matter whose welcoming arms might have invited us.

So we made it back to the base, largely by luck,
and the next day I was out of the Navy,
on a Trailways bus home.

1966

Crotalina*

Beware of entrance to a quarrel. – WILLIAM SHAKESPEARE

My chance encounter
with a creature
so reserved and lethal
dispels a history of myth:

a grassy patch in a forest road
and resting there,
an amber head, olive neck,
be-jewelled length.

That frozen undulation
would let me pass
to my hillside campsite,
unharmed and unaware.

But I see and freeze
in instant reflex,
sensing her with a shock,
my arm hairs raised.

Wide-eyed,
I edge mere inches nearer.
Her sleekness wrinkles.
She gains purchase.

Then begins
the tick-tick-tick
of beaded tail,
her minimal alarm.

Long I look,
and then I shy away,
chastened.
I move on to let us be.

Why do I write
she and *her*?
Because she was so fine,
so unimposing,

and oh, so
circumspect
in wise bewaring
of any quarrel.

199_

*Crotalinae, *derived from the Greek word for castanet, is the name of the sub-family of pit-vipers that includes rattlesnakes.*

Poem that Ends with the Word No

Tortured wanderer,
overextending yourself
on hot, black Florida asphalt
in wiggling confusion of heat waves!

Did you not raise reptilian eyes
to recognize the ultimate predator
coolly sighting a shotgun
at the head of your jeweled length?

Did not your nervous tongue
tell you how much more deadly
was the cold steel of that barrel
than the harmless warmth
of my idling engine at roadside?

Could you not have writhed madly
back into striking range,
become the devil legend says you are?

Could you not have shown
the serpentine malice
exemplified in Genesis garden,
and flung white-fanged jaws
against the mortal flesh of that man?

Could not I, arriving late,
have heard at least a buzz of rattle,
have seen you coil and tremble
against such a brainless death?

Could not I have been there
gazing in wonderment,
well ahead of him, to prod you,
both of us safe amid danger,
to edge you, urge you
out of other men's way?

Travel is fatal to prejudice . . .

Or could you not at least
have disappeared on your own
into the safe palmetto field
bordered by that byway?

Could you not have been swifter
than his ambitious trigger,
like the harmless black snakes
I frightened into the kudzu
of my childhood?

Could I not perhaps
have delayed him
with a casual word at least
before his macho spite
cracked the humid air,
blew your head utterly off,
stilled your dazed meandering,
and sent an oddly human trickle
of warmed snake blood
down your sleek neck?

No.

1988

The Bottlenose Dolphin

A funny thing happened
at the Gulfarium one August afternoon.

It's in Florida – Fort Walton Beach –
along the so-called Miracle Strip.

The boys just had to go:

They've got everything,
sting rays sea lions
and shows all day long
but Dad the dolphins are the best.
Let's go see 'em!

And so we did and so they were.

What I'm telling about happened
after the demonstration scuba dive
to the "Ocean Floor Adventure"
that transpired in a big, boxy aquarium
where sea turtles barracuda
grouper sea bass nurse sharks eels
catfish parrot fish dog-
fish all appeared to tolerate each other
and the diver.

It happened after the dolphin show as well.

I was strolling back
along their big, cylindrical tank.

Passing a small porthole,
I looked in on them for one last time,
and there they circled,
revved up yet
from their ace performance,
arching round their ring.

A curious one dove down –
large, keen eye glimpsing mine –
and then,
next time around,
stopped where I stood watching
and like a living second hand
ticked with that slick body
a whole clock-face of sleek, grey beauty
all around our still-point,
one wild, spinning eye
fixed on me,
mouth in natural grin.

197_

Coastal Scene

Amelia Island, Florida, April 2, 1986

Out on the wide Atlantic
white shrimp boats, like greedy pelicans,
reach down to scoop up catch.

Here extending out past surf,
a solid concrete pier
is lined by folk with fishing poles.

Spring sun and breeze,
undulating vees of seabirds
ride easy currents up the coastline.

Day of unimpeded peace.

Cumberland Island

January 1990

Live oak trunks twist,
undulate limbs upward,
and wiggle out to branches
tipped in tiny, shiny leaves.

Sinewy limbo dancers
swaying under and up to the sky,
they waver to the wind's tempo,
lit by the drums of evening sun.

Grounded easily
in their gyrating shadows,
warm in my bag sipping tea,
I rest like one of their seeds.

Green Flash

Higgs Beach, Key West, Florida, January 22, 2015

An illusion
as some say,
or is it a real, observable thing?

Science says it's real –
a prismatic effect
occurring under certain circumstances:

a sliver of sunlight
through just-right sky,
an accommodating atmosphere
at start or end of day,
an egg-yolk sun
that teases with the slightest arc
a bit above horizon,
air a perfect lens.

Sometimes,
those rare conditions being so,
most likely over water,
it will show a wide band
or ray of green,
I'm told.

This clear evening,
I stand watch at the setting sun
for any outside chance
to see some vague, amorphous,
slight chromatic shift
that might give me a claim
to having captured such a flash.

Sun was all but gone
beneath a rim of sea.

And then that flash!

A sharp, piercing green,
bright as if a traffic light
mere blocks away
had blinked a nanosecond,
bidding *Go!*

Or as if a starboard buoy,
set to keep the nighttime safe,
had winked to tempt a voyage
to where our star was going.

Gestures

Guadalajara, Mexico

Here's a hapless great-grandmother
ensconced like a Tara
on a busy sidewalk,

like the Roma I saw last year
on my tour of Spanish opulence.
I marvel again in passing
how such desperate folk can live.

You need not travel far to see them.

Often the frail arms are upraised,
leathery hands arched back,
arthritic fingers curving upward
past us surely, up to the heavens even,
up to the very throne of God,
holding hope and patience
like an empty cup.

Not really begging, though,
these old souls of meager expectation,
merely willing to receive,
humbled subjects
to anyone's perception
of chronic need.

Here now a year and continent away,
this same, care-worn woman,
Amerindian this time, I believe,
haunting my Gringo conscience again.

I think of the Roma
and so many others
I've dismissed for decades.

I take out a wad of pesos,
walk back my carefree tourist jaunt,
put crisp new bills in her hands
that curl round them in shocked joy,

then clutch my larger hand,
her ancient, cloudy eyes,
rheumy with all the history
of human suffering,
gazing up to mine.

Gracias! she exclaims
with a vice-like squeeze,
but the eyes say more.

So I dare to say it for us:
Gracias a Dios, Abuelita,
beaming down on her
as if I were humble,
reverent, wise.

A Dios she echoes
(not just *adios*)
before she lets me go.

But no –
I made that whole encounter up
including the part about God.
It's only what might well have been
or might yet be.

I rushed right on past that one too
to get myself a sumptuous dinner,
marveling again
how much the dollar buys
in Mexico this year.

2017

Deux Mec

Puerto Vallarta, Mexico

The popular pizzeria on the corner
is raucous and clattering tonight,
no table for one anyway,
so I stroll on to a classy new place.

With the half-priced peso lately
and this restaurant calm and spacious,
I take an elevated street-side table
with a smug overview of all the nightlife
that thrives in this buzzing *Zona Romantica*.

Here's one helluva party town
where rowdy appetites flock in winter
down from the cold and driven north
to gobble and guzzle cheap pizza and beer.

You haven't been here till you've seen
some oblivious young Gringo
prone on the cool sidewalk, circled
by the concerned or curious,
next to a glistening belly-full
his stomach has just rejected.

I was midway into my mild, finely sauced
fish filet whose French name escapes me,
when a golden-locked, blue-eyed Hans
fresh out of the von Trapp family,
appears at my table to stand at attention
and introduce himself as my chef.

I praise the meal to his blushing smile,
imagining I might somehow get him
to remove that white kitchen jacket,
sit down, and be my dinner friend this evening.

Before he retreats, I get him to tell me
he was schooled in Switzerland,
prompting me to dust off my French
about which he's more than gracious,
gently reminding me that *deux* means *two*, not *god,*
so that the name of the place is *Two Guys*, not *God-men*
(though if his partner should turn out
to have his striking looks and manners
I'd surely visit their shrine).

So euphoric in the evening's glow am I,
so encouraged by the perfect wine,
that I even eat the nasturtium flower
off an exquisite dish of ice cream and berries,
the culinary name of which I also forget.
(My friend who watches *Top Chef*
recently told me when I visited him here
each garnish on a plate should be edible.)

So utterly predisposed am I, in fact,
to be completely satisfied tonight
that I nonchalantly dispatch
with my little silver dessert fork
the microbial white wormlet
that must have escaped from the flower
to wriggle across a droplet of chocolate,
under which I carefully entomb it
with a discretion I deem fitting
on such a special occasion.

I only wish now I'd eaten it too.

2017

Flight of Fancy

Puerto Vallarta, Mexico

The sea's so calm this morning,
nibbling coyly at the beach
by my open-air breakfast table,
but the sea (and all that lies beneath it)
shifts itself just as it pleases.

Suppose the other guests and I
watch, unbelieving, a last little wave
recede and keep right on receding,
exposing beach we'd never seen before,
never even dreamed of seeing.

Old bones of long-sunk boats drip slick
green seaweed shocked in sunlight.
Dozens of fish flop out on drying sand,
gills gaping for something vital,
taken for granted till now, like us.

How long would we gaze on, amazed?
Would a curious boy trot down to investigate
some treasure suddenly laid bare?
Would frantic voices call him back in time?

Would we know, or would sirens scream
for us to drop our forks and our distractions?

Take nothing. Just run. Climb up higher!
Up the cobbled streets, quaint stairs of stone,
we'd stumble beneath oblivious bougainvillea,
abandon the unlucky left below, each one of us
desperate for a height that means survival –

before that little wave returned, all changed?

2017

Morning Meals

Puerto Vallarta, Mexico

Breeze eases off the bay
ruffling a feathered competition
of clattering black birds –
uniformed in iridescent sheen.

They scan the foot-printed sand
beneath a jumble of blue
canvas beach chairs,
empty now of international fellows
who in their sunlit lounging,
raucous drinking, eating yesterday
left crumbs the birds are scavenging
as I idly watch and peck
at my own breakfast.

Are they crows, ravens, grackles?
(I'm no ornithologist.)

And is the sand they swallow
along with the scraps they scarf
a hindrance or a help
with avian digestion –

or maybe, like this poem,
nothing at all to them?

2017

In the Shadow of the Moon

1.

The sticky-note above my desk
kept reminding me for over a year:

*Great American Eclipse
August 21, 2017*

I'd be sure to see it, make great plans,
get my guy to skip his work, go up with me,
join some observation group perhaps,
gather with friends right in its broad path,
whoop it up, go *Wow!* with all the others.

But then a grim political year crawled on
like the beast toward Bethlehem,
a nation-wide phenomenon
already dividing our continent
relentlessly down its midst,
blocking the brightest, enshrining
darkest fears and motivations
all across this land,
that was supposed to belong
to you and me.

Before it even got here,
this august, celestial event
loomed more like an ominous echo
of what's been going down
for months here – years in fact.
This coincident black-out,
warning us from high in midday sky,
will be nothing to celebrate.
I know why ancients feared them,
always ascribed dark meanings.
We might recognize this curse,
see to our sorrow its unfolding.

Still, routes will be choked
with air-conditioned pilgrims
desperate, unlike me,
for any available distraction.
I've seen a partial one before.
He'd never take a day off anyway.
Why swell that curious crowd?
Let others go ape over this if they will.
I'll see photos, video eventually.
For now I'll pan the whole hyped show.

     2.

But then the day rolls round.
And what is it urges me now
to fill a water bottle, stock a daypack,
hop in, head north on winding byways?
(Maybe the new-bought Honda
with latest bells and whistles?)

So I'm going after all
to get myself well into the shadow,
be one more eye-ball witness
to an unearthly loss of light,
an event blindly indifferent
to the sordid scenes down here
(however we might suffer them).

     3.

But where and when will the sun,
the moon, the earth – and I – all coincide?
Where will I park to get myself
under that miles-wide shadow?

Will I arrive at the place late?
Why did I not make those plans
for this once-in-a-lifetime moment?
(My own darkness sometimes stuns me!)

But let's see now.
If total eclipse begins to cover
northwest Tennessee at just past noon,
then crosses Nashville
perhaps an hour after that,
I'm making doubtful progress –
but wait, that's Central Time.
Will I keep this madcap rendezvous?

Be it as it may, western Carolina
under eastern Tennessee
is the likeliest spot to be.

So, up from sun-lit turns
and curves of blue highways weaving me on
toward Murphy, North Carolina,
tooling along in the new car's first big run,
passing gatherings of local folk
already staring up from yards,
some taken aback in lounge chairs,
angling faces up like heliotropes
in their special blind-man glasses,
I press swiftly onward.

4.

And then I take my chance,
swerve up onto a hilly hard-dirt lot,
park shiny green machine aimed south,
and lacking the recommended lenses,
punch holes in a sheet of cardboard
with an old ice pick I brought.

And there they are: shiny fingernail clips
of sunlight beamed through open moon roof
onto a scrap of black paper.

Meanwhile, aloft,
two ponderous great sky-ships are underway

undeniably easing past each other peacefully
with plenty of space between
their two great spheres of movement.
These tiny curves of light that prove it
seem to be unchanging though.
I thought I might detect
some thickening or slimming.

I hazard a direct glance
up into the overhead glare
and instantly think better of that,
shy back to check on paper
the images pinholes are making.

Are these minute crescents waxing?
Is the whole eclipse
already past its prime,
or is it still a waning light
about to be eclipsed completely?

I see it now. They're shrinking.
Those tiny golden almost-arcs
are absolutely thinner than they were.

                5.

Exit my driver door,
step out in eerie mid-day grey
drape-like around an empty road,
feel an unaccustomed cool
on summer skin.

A brief cacophony of fireworks
explodes from somewhere out of sight.
An unseen voice from elsewhere yells,
Don't make noise! Just enjoy it!
Both outbursts have their place,
but more than any counterpoint
I welcome restored quiet now,

this extraordinary, twilit mid-day,
I among the silent few
watching in solitude
a show unlike all others.

I hear no sudden crickets,
see no cattle stumbling
back toward their barns.
I don't have to duck a sudden volley
of agitated bats.

I do though raise receptive eyes to see
a round, black silhouette of face
with golden hair afire –
and she looks livid!

I stare right back,
unblinking, hypnotized,
whole seconds safe from danger.

Then the moon mask that slid so easy on
glides right on off,
solar stage light glinting down again,
blinding back to us from where it hid
the dazzling diamond ring –
and soon an ordinary afternoon again.

But that came only after
in the eerie, still-point dark
I observe a sky of constellations
bright as midnight,
spot the Hunter when I'd never seen him
lead his dogs before,

then gaze to the west
where high and clear as day
Venus beams, unblemished and unjudging,
radiant,
above mundane preoccupations.

Tunneling

traveling through the pandemic

. . . dark is what brings out your light . . .
– ROBERT FROST, *"Take Something Like a Star"*

Eyes are still adjusting
to lack of light.
Can we be bioluminescent?

Irises expand their lenses,
but this is a pure-blind path
foot-felt before us.

We're as if entombed living
in a darkened heart of pitch,
ghosts that still keep going

here where dampness
only aggravates the blight.
Here a drip, drip, drip

of subterranean drops
from a chilling vault aloft.
No eagerness, no pleading

conjures least light here
where none's to see, just black
along these necessary rails.

Flashes, scintillations.
Blips on retinas, nothing
more than eye tinnitus.

Flickers of actual light?
Foxfire, glowworm,
glimmers maybe.

But tunneling, by definition,
ends. When we *are* borne,
even out of a shaft like this,

to see, initially at least,
no better lights, not even stars –
we know they're up there.

2020

There are more things in heaven and earth, Horatio, than are dreamed of in your philosophy.

– WILLIAM SHAKESPEARE

Rude Awakening

Well, we grow *up*,
you know. We rock along
with all the answers
for a long or little while.

Then, something, *Whoa!*
suddenly doesn't fit
yesterday's plan or expectation,
and there we are, stumped

by our *daimonion*
like that loveable old Socrates
who claimed that all he knew
was that he didn't know.

2012

A Time & Place for Everything?

What is mind? No matter. What is matter? Never mind.
– GEORGE BERKLEY

Recall the clever old conundrum,
the one about whether you can know
the whole world is really out there somewhere
or whether you're just indulging
some totally convincing hallucination
conjured up inside your own fictitious head?

Consider too the theory of a Big Bang, before which
this great everywhere was a timeless, spaceless dot
of infinite mass and energy – which also recalls
the curious notion that space was only invented
to get things all spread out, time another wizard's trick
to turn the cosmos into a sequence, not an endless now.

Future's a hope, a fear, an expectation;
past is a shifting, fleeting reminiscence (or regret),
and now this timeless crux we call the present
seems only the swiftest stroke of a virtual brush
painting along the fantasy surface of things,
turning future faster than instantly to memory or loss.

Assuming all that to be likely (or even conceivable)
how on earth can a popping pot of red geraniums,
gradually blooming away here on a solid oak table
in glittery morning sun – or for that matter I myself,
lolling through my scribbling in a leather La-Z-Boy,
be known to exist – at any place, any time – at all?

2017

Sources of Truth

One cannot know truth
But he can embody it. – WILLIAM BUTLER YEATS

Viewpoint is as given
as our stature
or our skin.

Reasons, words
may justify,
twist, or convince.

Knowledge, though
is carnal, deeper
than the mind.

The heart, the gut,
the bones as well,
bear all the truth we find.

2018

Plato's Sun

Those who seek for idols cannot know the star is there.
– A COURSE IN MIRACLES

There is a crack, a crack in everything. That's how the light gets in.
– LEONARD COHEN

        1.

If I'm to see the moon,
and not the finger pointing,
am I not to see beyond the moon as well?

Isn't the moon, or at least my image of it,
just another finger pointing further?

In other words,
if Plato's prisoner
can come unchained to clamber out
from his cave and into the light of day,
doesn't the plain light of day
turn out to be another cave?

        2.

Once in a guided meditation group,
we were directed by our leader,

*Imagine yourself going
to seek the wise one in the cave;
and when you meet,
ask your one earth-shattering question.*

So, resting with eyes closed,
I enter a dark hole in a cliff,
make my imagined way inside,

detour around outcrops,
squeeze between cracks,

slog through sludge and water,
clamber over boulders,
leap across crevices,
and crawl on my belly
till I face
an absolute dead end.

3.

After catching my breath,
I grab a hefty loaf of stone
and hammer at the wall of rock
rising to block me.

Gradually it gives
in a clatter of fragments.

Yellow light shines through,
sunlight
filling an enormous room.

Gazing up, mouse-like, I see myself,
an equally enormous child
dancing happily
as any laughing Buddha
to music I've never heard.

I forget to ask my question.

1995

Chuang Tzu & the Butterfly*

I think therefore I am.
But do I *indisputably* think
or do I only *think* I do –
and even were I sure of that,
would I be *what* I think I am?

And if I only *think* I think,
Isn't that a rabbit hole
(if rabbits had such holes)
of only more assumptions?
(You see where that's going!)

We have to start – and end –
at arbitrary points.
Even Socrates himself
knew only what was likely
(or so it seemed to him).

2019

This legend refers to the Chinese emperor who dreamed he was a butterfly, in a dream so vivid that when he woke he thought he might really be a butterfly – dreaming he was a man now.

She Spoke Slowly, Seated like a Lotus

You are more than any speculation.
Be free to breathe a long, heartfelt sigh.
Relinquish strife and pettiness,
bitterness, all your fear or anger.
Ease your body. Free your mind.
Home yourself to a deep, calm core.

You are the unfathomable crux
of cosmic energies. You mirror
these vast forces, reflect them,
own them, *are* these intricacies:
thinking, seeing, touching, smelling,
ultimately *being* an envisioned world:

Lavender dew-dripping iris at dawn,
tuft of Kelly-green moss by a waterfall,
crystalline tower gilded at sundown,
pearl of moon pillowed in cloud,
apple-face of a wide-eyed infant.
All of these phenomena, all of you.

Be – larger than any contingency.
Breathe a deep, heartfelt sigh, be
lazy even. No anxiety, no fear of suffering
through, no sharpness in a shoulder, no regrets.
No. Ease your body. Free your mind.
Home yourself to your deep, calm core.

1989

Parable

I'm ambling down the beach
and everything's just fine –
surf mumbling, sun glinting
off water and sand.

Suddenly I stumble headlong
down this cavernous hole
I didn't see coming.

High walls are calving into slush
at the bottom where I'm sprawled.

I stand, knee-deep and sinking,
helpless fingers stretched to a callous sky.

Surf is slapping closer.

I claw against my trap
bringing down an avalanche of sand.

My two options now are
drowning or suffocating,
maybe a measure of both,
depending on the wetness
of the slurry I die in.

Then I see the rope,
tie an end around a stone
I hadn't noticed either,
throw it out,
haul myself up,
and stroll off down the beach,
surf mumbling, sun glinting.

1986

The Myth of Sisyphus

The birds they sang at the break of day.
Start again, I heard them say. – LEONARD COHEN

I for one will still start up,
after a dark and rainy downcast day,
when a rainbow arcs unexpectedly
across a steely bright afternoon sky

That first late-winter jonquil,
defying the cold and dark,
has always been a sign of hope.
The last maple leaves sky-diving
down the autumn air
all wave a whimsical good-bye.

I still gawk in mind-boggling awe
at someone's innocent baby born,
however many grow to be monsters,
however many heroes die tilting at them.

When Barbra croons, *Some-wheeere* . . . .
I'm sure in my sappy, happy heart,
despite all *Breaking News* to the contrary,
such a haven really does prevail somewhere
with a more congenial climate
and a welcoming immigration policy.

Doors close, other doors open,
The long arc of justice, and all of that.

Still, I can't quite contradict
(or agree with either)
Edna St. Vincent Millay
who famously noted,

It is not true that life
is one damn thing after another;
it's one damn thing over and over,

which brings us right back
to tireless old Sisyphus
still shouldering his stone
(surely not so gigantic
as in those cartoons we've seen).

Consider the thought-worthy view
of French philosopher, Albert Camus,
who fought fascism in the '40s
before dying young in an auto crash:

One must imagine Sisyphus happy.

2018

Errand

Be wet with a decent happiness. – ROBERT CREELEY

Our neighbor-friends
flew off this morning,
this time to Puerto Rico,

asking us to please
see to their mail
till they get back next week.

I slipped on my Crocs
(green and embossed
in faux crocodile skin,
I'll have you know)

strolled lazily out our back door
into an unexpected patter of rain
falling into our neighborhood
like a natural baptism.

I thought of how we scurry
to escape the slightest wet
as if we all had silly hairdos
teased up high and vulnerable
to anything less than shiny weather.

So I decided not to rush.
I strolled on slowly
letting the spring drizzle
tickle my skin a little.

I remembered
Sink your energy
as I was advised to do,
allowed my belly to go slack,
drooped my shoulders back
and breathed my way serenely,

chest forward,
across the misty asphalt
to their mailbox –
as if there were no need
to get there
or get to anywhere at all.

And need there was none.
The mail hadn't arrived,

which is not at all to say
my meditative errand
was a waste of time.

2019

The Book of Truth

And take upon 's the mystery of things,
As if we were God's spies. – WILLIAM SHAKESPEARE

Mankind cannot bear very much reality. – T. S. ELIOT

If there were such a marvelous volume
filled with answers to any and all possible questions,
mysteries solved, superstitions
and conspiracy theories debunked (or validated)
by some ultimate authority on everything,
every word in its pages undeniably true,

and if, against all likelihood,
it were ever entrusted to me,
I'd start by learning what really happened
to the lost Roanoke Colony,
and then I'd find out the fate of Earhart and Hoffa.

I'd discover why my great-grandfather Perryman
left England for Georgia centuries ago
(to die young, of measles and pneumonia, in our war).
Also what he hoped for all his progeny,
including me.

and look up the formula
for a Unified Field Theory
to see if it really is astoundingly simple
after all.

I'd vet quite a few political claims and denials,
take a hard look at a certain crook's tax returns,
shine light on his shady dealings,
read what Putin has on him –
and promptly alert the *Times*,
the *Post*, *CNN* and *ABC*.

But there are more important truths:
I'd recover all the lore lost
when the library at Alexandria burned,
find out what cultures with no written records
could bequeath to our advantage now,
see where royal tombs are languishing undetected
under desert sands or jungle vines.

I might even dare to look up
the cause and time of my demise,
especially if it reveals ways to postpone it.

If, that is, I did somehow
have that book of all books
which, as we do know, does not exist
and wouldn't be in my mere hands if it did.

Meanwhile, has anyone seen my cellphone?
Would someone please call it for me?

2019

In my dreams the most charming forms have come to console and to cheer me.

– JOHANN WOLFGANG von GOETHE

Flying Dreams

You broke free from the cage . . . and flew. – RUMI

I used to gaze beyond an open hatch
and promptly take my flight,
but there were hazards from the start.
I flapped tentative wings in fear
just to clear strung power lines,
felt myself clawed at like Tweety Bird
by wingless feline predators,
got tangled in treetops, trapped in lime.

Or else I'd wing it all so wonderfully
I'd wake amazed to be an earthbound boy.
I'd hurry out to fan my unfledged arm-wings
in the morning yard, attempting the air.
By the time I heard the technical term,
I also had some knack for navigating
up and down my fluctuating altitudes.

But as a wise guide told me then,
*In time your lows will be as high
as your highs are already,
and those highs – well, pardon this cliché,
but the sky's your limit, man.*

Oh, I could crash again – and burn – today.
What goes up, forgive me this one too,
must yes indeed come down again.
But I'm an old bird now, with steady eyes
except when low-blown clouds obscure my view.

1998

If You Must Take Notes

That's it, in a patient voice admonishing me,
all I remember from a dream last night.

I was engaged in something pleasant,
probably with you as usual,

but where it was or what it was eludes me.
Just that one conditional clause echoes to say,

You own the mystique of this moment.
If you must annotate it, as you often try to do,

then write this poem.

2014

What Do We Call Dreams like These?

I'm a digger in Death Valley
down past Coke cans, chip bags,
down past brazen armor
of old conquistadors,
down to iridescent raku
Amerindian ceramics,
perfect and scintillating in sunlight.
Then deeper I delve
to unearth a hidden wonder:
the Starburst Crystal,
a frozen fountain of clear quartz.
I place it gingerly on the home piano.
All the clan admires this find.

From a crimson church carpet
where we lie fetal, as our yogi shows,
we rise, join hands, and circle
to commence a holy chant.
I *Shhhhh* the whispering at my ear
that would explain each word.
My voice begins to form the sacred song.
I know its undeniable truth.

Mid-center an ice-white Merlin's cave
glitters the crystal lens
I sight through to see
the whole kaleidoscopic world
merge into harmony.

Son Scott and I stroll arm in arm
to fish from the dock in Cedar Key.
My late and favorite aunt, deceased in 1989,
strides up with rod and bucket,
bids us welcome, and exclaims,
Yeah, here it is 1998 and I'm still catching fish!

1994

Sweet Dream*

Mauve sky silhouettes
a shrimp boat, a dockside bar.
Foraging pelicans swoop offshore
in lazy wheels and ribbons.

Morning breeze warms
me with a salty savor.
A scribble of palmetto trees
delineates the far horizon.

Soon all the bay glitters
in celebratory sunrise,
casting a bright patina
over the whole scene.

This simple dream releases
such wells of feeling,
so comforting, they wet
my face and wake me.

1977

*I used to lead courses in "Dream Analysis" where students recorded and shared their dreams and decided on useful meanings. We all knew the name of a terrible dream (maere, from Old English, refers to an incubus, goblin, or evil spirit), and those were always revealing and valuable – but no one knew a common name for the opposite sort of dream, a euphoric one like this one (which was unmistakably set in Cedar Key, Florida, where I had so many good times with family and friends).

In one of my groups, we eventually settled on the simple name "sweet dreams" and decided that we could learn as much from them as from the others, even though the bad ones can be more memorable. By valuing and studying the sweet dreams, we also found that we began to have them more often.

Waking Dream

for Claude*

I'm young in an ice-bound province.
(It isn't from history this comes.)
I struggle to parrot a steel dialectic,
but with soft silver tongue.

I see winter rush onto the steppes
driving merciless gusts of snow,
overtaking late-falling leaves,
weaving blankets of cold.

I gaze up at lavender mountains,
ranges that hold us down in our pain
like hopeless, herded animals,
clawing roots from a barren plain.

Cold-featured men, brothers of mine,
revolting now! Fixed bayonets
and quick-gushing blood
on a white gauze of snow, yet

a long chain of train cars snakes away,
black engine rising through the white land,
(powerful artifact of its own revolution)
leaving the carnage below, and

wee, waxen leaf from a winter-black stem,
and a well-kept promise under that snow
of egg-yellow jonquils flocked on hillsides,
drinking the ice as they grow.

1976

**My father's younger brother lied and claimed he was old enough to help fight in the "Great War." He ended up in the American Expeditionary Force sent to support White Russians against the Reds in Asia during their civil war. He was assigned the duty of guarding a garbage dump and firing over the heads of* *starving local folk who would slip into the camp to steal potato peelings, coffee grounds, and other salvageable scraps.*

With a history of then-undiagnosed schizophrenia, Claude suffered a breakdown and was sent home to a miserable life in and out of a government mental hospital in Augusta, Georgia, until his early death in 1950.

I felt almost possessed by this "vision" one winter morning and hurried to get it typed up. Besides reminding me of my uncle's awful experience that I'd heard about second-hand, the poem was inspired by the film, Dr. Zhivago, *which also had an impact on me.*

The Dreamer

That castle is a lofty royal pile.
He prefers the servants' quarters though.

A free but unobtrusive boy,
he watches bustling servants
cut up potatoes, pluck hens,
and kindly tolerate his presence
while singing ballads in curious dialect.

He sits transfixed of an evening,
arms clasping pale calves,
self-contained as a winter seed,
staring into the bright flickers
of a cheerful kitchen fire,

He ignores the long, dull lessons of the day,
secretly consoled with not-yet-proven merit.

After all, he's merely a foundling here.

Budding knights with bolder expectations
strive among themselves to win the jousts
and all those other tedious games of prowess.

They pull his hair in passing,
wrestle him down, and call him queer.
They laugh in scorn that such a churl
should even live to crowd their table.

But he has visions, Maytime afternoons,
of pardoning their crass aggressions.

Some dawn he might lead them
to the glen where a red fox darts
and tends her mewling kits
in a hidden cleft among the mossy stones.
Then such creatures would not be their quarry.

And how the dreams come round!

Certain nights a greybeard sage appears
to penetrate his thin disguise with fire-coal eye
and name him heir apparent to the realm.

One night he grips the legendary sword
and frees it, holds it, haft up, above his head;
then wakes, hands clenched, as if in prayer,
tangled amid the covers of his bed.

198_

The Stillness

Weave a circle round him thrice. – SAMUEL TAYLOR COLERIDGE

At the still point of the turning world, there the dance is. – T. S. ELIOT

Just now I dreamed I strolled
along my way, at ease, in awe
among tall, swaying trees
on a natural, sun-drenched path.

I imagined then the fine words
I'd be sure to muster
soon as I woke
to convey the perfection
of this supreme, green-golden
scene enclosing me.

The poem I'd write about it
would be like rare ones
I revisit with a shiver,
hairs rising on my neck
as I take in the flawlessness
of some poet's imagery –
Keats' warm beaker, for example,
With beaded bubbles
winking at the brim.

My poem would show
how a slight spring breeze
settled to rest around me,
countless leaves ceasing their flutter
as a quiet, steady rhythm built
while morning sun beamed
onto my upturned face.

And at this one privileged crux
in the pitiless ratcheting out of time,
all became eternal harmony

resonating interdependently –
like the beads in Indra's net.*

Waking though to ordinary daylight,
I can't conjure up such magic here.
I can only struggle to hint
at how supremely marvelous
that dream this morning was
and is in glowing memory,
how amazing any poem that did it justice
would have to try to be.

2012

*Indra's net is a Buddhist metaphor for the concept of the interconnectedness of all things in time and space. It is imagined as an infinite, three-dimensional net extending throughout the universe with, at each intersection of its threads, a crystal bead that reflects every other bead in the net, as well as every reflection of every reflection without end – a little like the facing mirrors in a barber shop, only far more intricate

Cut Off Head, Spite Face?

In this dark dream, my worthy friend
stands outside his home, cheerful,
on his lawn, slicing his own
head off with a hunting knife.

He's so sure of what he's doing,
I so deferential to his good sense,
it doesn't cross my sleeping mind
to say he might rethink his action.

The first cut's not so lethal,
a light stroke across the front
of his neck, bleeding, of course,
but apparently with little pain,
his face still in a confident grin.

It's as though this butchering
will go as planned with good result,
without a penalty. I watch, amazed
at such courage, such purpose,
no thought of his foolhardiness.

But then the tougher work begins.
He'll need to slice his way
through windpipe, jugulars,
even solid vertebrae somehow.
He'll die before the deed is done,

one that's now become more grisly,
gristly, with ruddy gouts flecking
my clean white shirt. I stare transfixed
by such a tragic nonchalance.

And then, as can chance in dreams,
it's my own neck severed, my remorse
for thinking I could carry this
to any sensible completion.

I stumble up into the house
hand clasped over the hemorrhaging,
seeing belatedly, terrified,
what a mortal blunder this has been.

At last released, as we normally are,
awakened out of my subconscious horror,
my neck wonderfully intact,
I escape that lurid scene.

I rest now in my safe, warm bed
to wonder what may have moved
either him or me to such a deed,
and what that trial could teach us.

2015

Remembering Dreams

This morning I woke
as certain as ever
that last night I dreamed –
something pleasant,
not one of those dreams
I'm released from relieved
that my cellphone works
to summon the help
I desperately needed
but no longer need,
that my car's where I left it,
that at last I've escaped
simply by waking
from unbearable guilt
for unspeakable crimes
I can never define,
though the guilt is all too real.

But I just can't recall
last night's nice-
enough dream.
I know sleep studies show
we have to dream
through cycles of REM
every night of our lives,
dreams remembered or not –
or else we forfeit
our waking sanity.

Then too, we all dream
our wide-awake dreams,
consciously created,
the ones we'd die
on life's extending vine

In my dreams the most charming forms . . .

if we couldn't pursue
and somehow sustain –
the learnings and loves
that give our lives meaning,
the dutiful labors
we carry out daily,
remember with pride,
even ones we abandoned,
ones we forgot,
forgiving ourselves
for our failures.

2020

*Nothing is at last sacred
but the integrity
of your own mind.*

– RALPH WALDO EMERSON

Dress-up

Because we cannot know all truth
and since we never will,
because the truths we think we know
amount to almost nil,

we'll gild our little baby truths
in swaddling clothes and gems.
We'll dress them up and trick them out
according to our whims.

And, oh, those ancient, sacred truths
(the ones that hardly were),
what fine furs we've furnished them,
and how they make a stir.

The peace those gaudy dogmas claim
lies down a bloody path,
and yet we kneel to kiss their rings;
we kill on their behalf.

I'll take each little truth as is
to see how well he grows.
Like everyone who thinks and feels,
I'll dress him thus and so.

But when he dares to prance and strut
and claim some godly lore,
I'll strip him down and scrub him clean –
and shove him out the door.

2006

Faith

It is true, I never assisted the sun materially in his rising, but, doubt not, it was of the last importance only to be present at it. – HENRY DAVID THOREAU

I believe
in a great beyond
the precious little
I think I know,

and rarely do I object
to another person's
sincere profession
of faith.

It's the presumption
of certainty that disturbs me,
the effort to claim, beyond evidence,
infallibility.

Render the infinite finite.
Square the circle.
Calculate *pi* to conclusion.
Out-riddle the Sphinx.
Harness the whirlwind.
Then tell me all you know.

Little did fearful,
faithful ancients know
their fires and evergreens
did not lure back the sun,

but like our friend Thoreau
they thrived
assuming voluntarily some role
in all this Mystery.

2018

Miracles & Gods

1.

If a miracle is anything
believed to be a miracle –
amazing, wonderful,
unexplained –
then no proof is necessary,
so said the infamous Mark Twain.

If a religion you don't believe in is superstition,
but *bona fide,* eternal truth if you do believe it,
you see how we might misconstrue one another,
especially in matters so numinous.

2.

Guest-speaking to a mythology class
of attentive ninth-graders once,
I claimed the tale of Icarus,
while neither factual nor possible,
was yet quite true.

One girl's mother called the principal:

Is this man promoting another religion?

He politely, wisely referred her to me.

I said to her what I'd said to them:
We know no human ever flew
or fell in such a way,
but still the danger
to a beloved child
who wanders too far
despite a parent's warning
is undeniably real – and true.
This satisfied the lady, so she said.

Nothing is at last sacred . . .

3.

Hearing a tap of the brass door knocker,
I open to two cropped, teen-faced
Mormon "elders" on their mission.
I almost give my usual
No thank you
and almost close them out
as I have many others,

but free and idle, home alone,
I see faces so sincere and hopeful,
I welcome them in and give them water.

Do you know Jesus?

Yes, I say, trying to imagine
what that can mean
to them and even to me.

Do you read the Bible?

Yes, I say, honestly enough.

What do you read?

I take the liberty then
of reading them my favorite passage:
King James, I Corinthians 13.

That's nice, one young elder says.

Then I read them the same passage, *RSV*.
That makes a lot more sense, the other exclaims.

Do you have The Book of Mormon? one wants to know.

No, I tell them, so they kindly give me one.
I open to a famous painting,
the profile of Jesus (that looks Scandinavian).

I turn the page and there He is again,
robed in white, shining bright, enlightening
dusky tribes gathered round him.
Jesus Christ visits the Americas, the caption says.

Did Jesus visit the New World? I wonder.

Yes, is their cautious reply.

Well, I say, remembering my Twain,
is that a historical fact – or a miracle?

A miracle, they both assure me.

OK, if that's the case, we need no proof at all.

4.

Joseph Campbell, who followed his bliss
and published *The Hero with a Thousand Faces*,
gave a lecture once, I'm told,
at the end of which a proverbial little old lady
stood to challenge him.

*Mr. Campbell, I was told you are an atheist.
I came to see for myself tonight,
and I do believe you* are *an atheist.*

Madam, he reportedly replied,
*anyone who believes in as many gods as I do
could* never *be an atheist.*

We should not assume. however,
that such a clever answer left that lady satisfied.

201_

Praise for Corn

If a child asked for bread, would any of you offer a stone instead?
– MATTHEW 7:9

One morning
    in the leafy green ocean
        the honeycomb of the corn's beautiful body
            is sure to be there. – MARY OLIVER

I was shucking a couple of ears to boil just now,
unlike busier folk these days
who buy them already shucked, cobbed –
if not canned, frozen, or pressed into chips.

As I worked, I wandered back mentally,
almost nostalgically, to ponder
the countless centuries when corn was,
and for that matter still is,
a staple of the human diet in this our "New World."

I thought about how dependably
pulling off a few pale green husks and golden silks
has always exposed those toothsome rows
of plump kernels to our anticipating gaze,
available for our sustenance and satisfaction.

I thought too that someone more or less like me,
eons past, must have had a similar thought.
She must in fact have given thanks in an ancient way
to what she might have called the Great Spirit,
thanks for something so inexplicably reliable,
so generous to this day, never once stunning us
with hard little rows of pebbles instead.

She would have so appreciated
the growth of the corn she'd tended all season long
(or in my modern case, trusted someone else to tend)
instead of a blighted, withered crop
that would have left her hapless folk to starve.

So I'm uncommonly glad and grateful
to have two good portions of corn here today
to boil and butter and salt and chomp
right down to their cobs at my leisure,
besides two good, imaginative ears to hear
that suppliant those ages ago as she offered
what I suspect may have been her prayer:

Oh vast, mysterious Source of all good things
received by my people here below,
may all of us be ever mindful of You, ever grateful.
May we strive daily to be worthy
of Your perennial bounty.

2013

To Whom It May Concern

I have a number of reasonably happy friends
who apparently, even in a pinch,
have hardly given You a serious thought,
much less a prayer, for years on end.
And I have to admit, I lose touch too,
though You're never quite out of mind.

There was a time when a local miracle would have done
to make me Your devotee once again – an embalmed relative
waking from his coffin pillow during the service,
a check in the mail for the exact amount of an overdue bill,
even just one little rose blooming in frozen January.

But no, You've always veiled yourself like Shakespeare
behind all these lovely but credible manifestations;
and a deity who even pretends to obey natural laws
that a clever human can discover (or invent)
is no god at all, as far as I can tell.

I know it hasn't always been that way:
Vishnu, Jehovah, Allah, Christ – marvelous presences, yes.
But they hardly move us the way they once did.
And don't think for one minute I'm retreating
into that holy womb of oneness again, either.

What I want is nothing less than utter awe and wonder:
livable rapport with those perfidious Russians,
a global community reconciling our human tribes,
one of those close encounters we've all been waiting for,
an end at last to these damned fits of doubt and depression.

Oh, I know you've heard all this a million times before;
I get this way myself, almost every winter.
And the only answer you ever come up with . . . is spring.

1976

Heavens

Accept the holy instant. – A COURSE IN MIRACLES

First there's the one we've all heard about:
the wing-and-harp one
no one imagines much these days.

Then there's an abstract Eastern one
for which we're trained to want no form
the mind can conjure,
where, as in the old adage,
we become the water
that glides harmlessly
right over the cliff
and
down
the
abyss
to flow on forever.

Maybe there's another heaven
well beyond our ordinary ken
where all of us living and dead
are numinously reunited and reconciled
for all eternity.

For me, there's this one
where that fairy-godmother aunt
and I rock once more
and chatter on into the Southern night
on her cool screened porch
to a chorus of katydids and tree frogs
in the live oaks and cedars outside,
one where I watch her hop up,
smack a trespassing mosquito
between her palms,
and show me with a scowl
the awful blood it sapped.

Then she'll settle back into her rocker
to go right on telling
how her dad walking home
from the train stop one afternoon
in Villa Rica, Georgia,
got struck by a bolt of lightning –
and lived!
to get up and make it
the rest of his way home
with only a big, black burn
on the calf of his leg!
Now feature that! she'll exclaim.

I know the heaven where you and I
lean together, still,
over the rail of a little bridge
in easy summer rain
that patters both our names
in Maytime monotone,
brailling a tea-dark pond
with its indecipherable message –
where white lotus flowers rise
motionless above their flat green pads
reaching maiden-white, pearl-dripped fingers
to a welcome sky lover.

Now already and at last,
we have this very heaven,
right here now wherever we are
amid some vasty what-not –
this odd-ball little planet mind
where light and leaves and love are –
this one I can't begin to tell.

1995

Acts of God

Is God willing to prevent evil, but not able?
Then he is not omnipotent.
Is he able, but not willing?
Then he is malevolent.
Is he both able and willing?
Then whence cometh evil?
Is he neither able nor willing?
Then why call him God? – EPICURUS

Unlike broken mirrors,
the garden hose came
with a seven-year warranty
against bad luck –

a limited warranty though,
for defects in workmanship,
and just in the course
of normal home use –
but not, it stipulates,
for *Acts of God,*

which got me wondering
whether God acts
in certain cases
but not in others.

All power,
wisdom, goodness,
and presence
should, it seems
to my mere mind,
provide benevolence
and management
in every situation
from the swirling
of our busy cosmos
to the rising of the sun
on ripening corn –

even including
the care of a garden hose
left in that summer sun –
turned off, mind you,
but the nozzle shut tight,
said hose neglected,
I concede, warming
the water swelling inside,

not so much unlike
the pressure in a vein,
that burst a lethal aneurism
near the end of my hose,
unsealing it, sealing its fate.

Walmart let me return it,
which says a little something
about commercial benevolence.
The ninety days were up,
and admittedly I did ignore
expressed warnings
not to leave it unattended.

It's been hot as blazes
here this summer,
especially on the sunny
south side of the house
where my hose was hanging.

But enough about hoses.
What about God?
Does His inscrutable plan
provide leukemia for infants,
visit a painful demise
on my blameless friend,
not to mention
sending the flood that ruined
my downstairs carpet recently?

Is it the curse of fathers' sins,
or do the worst of things
just *seem* to be bad?
(Thank you, Sir.
May I please have another?)

Might we not appreciate
the genuine good we get,
without such glaring
counterpoints?

I'd sure love to give that a try,
but maybe I'd get *too* satisfied.

Oh, I know,
He moves mysteriously
His wonders to perform.
But if I dared to work that way,
my warranty would soon be gone.

2011

Wise Faith

Just as my life-long best friend liked to predict,
the sun came up again this morning.

I suggested to another good friend (agnostic like me)
that even such a prediction is still a confession of faith.

He claimed to truck with none of that fanciful stuff,
preferring facts, science, reality – common sense!

But that same oldest friend I mentioned first,
unapologetic rationalist that he was as well,

allowed, *I'm grateful. I just don't know who to thank,*
as if gratitude always required a designated recipient.

The debate isn't really about having faith though, is it,
but rather about how and where it's most wisely placed.

If I marvel in amazement and humbly thank
some vast, inscrutable *je ne sais quoi*

that nevertheless sustains me here for years,
while you kneel and pray in Jesus' name

to a personal, all-loving God
who hears you clearly and responds;

if a Buddhist nun in Thailand stops her digging
to relocate the worm she dared not sever,

out of some quaint faith she'd accepted early on,
something about compassion for all living creatures;

if every one of us here on this spinning ball
got out of bed this morning

trusting,
resting utmost, purblind confidence

in whatever it may be that gets us going
on with whatever lives

we've found it in our minds
and hearts and sinews to trust and pursue –

is it really any matter worth debating,
is it not in simplest terms one motivation?

Or, as yet another best friend told me decades ago,
Life is a maze with one exit. Why rush to get through it?

That would be true for me today,
if only a bloom or two might grace my path,

I muse idly, glancing out my upstairs study window
and seeing by chance – or not – the tall indigo glads

gradually reaching their way
up and out to bloom again this sunny-cold morning,

right there beside our front walk,
just as each year we've trusted they would.

2018

*It's all a draft
until you die.*

– ELLEN BRYANT VOIGT

What Tiresias* Knew

Life defined, delimited by dying,
however dreaded or postponed,
has meaning for us then.

Only then
is it a treasured gem,
not rare but transitory.

Without limitation, definition,
life infinite must be and be
into passionless eternity.

Not so much that brevity is best.
It's simply everything
we know and can with courage hold.

197_

In Greek myth, Tiresias was granted a life that lasted many generations but did not keep him from continuing to age.

Practice

As your raft approaches the waterfall, become the water.
– BUDDHIST MAXIM

                  1.

I've tried it more than once:
stripped, reclining
in a dreamy tub of hot water,
no workday rush to distract me,
drenched washcloth over my face,
I exhale with a sigh,
sink back into prenatal inertia,
deep, deep, deep . . . .

Pretty soon, I'm urged
by an age-old instinct: *Breathe!*
Can't!
Cloth sucks snug,
masks onto nose, mouth, face
with a ghastly hissing in
to form an air-tight seal.

So I simply relax and settle
for the air I still have in me,
then let the rest go too,
be empty as a meditating monk.

Eventually I poke my tongue out
to see if it might make a vent.

It can't!

Here I am, paralyzed, terminal,
suffocating, can't even scream!
This is death-panic,
and it's not nice at all.

*Lord, let me live
or be done with this*,
I fantasize.

I let go even more,
determine to want nothing,
go limp, back to the Mother –
back further, to not being at all.
(*Give up the ghost*,
as the old folks used to say.)

But something beyond
mere dogged will
won't give up at all,
blocks that evasion,
just *has* to save me again
(from what? for what?).

Is this how we might die?

Suppose I couldn't snatch the cloth
away and gulp another precious lungful
(which of course I do, instantly
ending my weird bath-time play).

What if I couldn't postpone my end,
or prolong my living one more time,
and I'm far beyond help,
can't call for it,
but not yet quite beyond
unbearable, unspeakable suffocation?
How long before it lets me go?

              2.

That 86-year-old spinster aunt of mine,
who lived and loved life
and had more horse sense
than all the rest of us,

dreaded the endgame,
but not its end.

She was no conventional believer,
but she revised the old bedtime prayer:

Now I lay me down to sleep.
If I should die before I wake,
thank you, thank you!

3.

I met a fellow once
with an incredible story
he claimed was true,
about his hippie friend in Florida
who lived to scuba dive.

After endless months
of terminal, debilitating illness,
the guy just disappeared.

Eventually
they found his diving bag
near one of those deep,
cold Florida springs.
Someone suited up
and dove down
to look for him.

There,
over a hundred feet below
the shallow surface of things,
weighted onto a sandy floor,
discarded tank and gear
set neatly at his side,
ghost of a smile on his lips
and wide shut eyes,
he sat in a lotus pose –

cooler and more blissful
than any breathing Buddha.

Did he simply relax,
inhale the cold, thick fluid
instead of ordinary daytime
air he'd grown so tired of taking?

Chill out?

Become the icy deep?

How much practice
would it take
to learn to go that way?

1999

Bucket Lists

Effort and expectation, and desire,
And something evermore about to be. – WILLIAM WORDSWORTH

I'm not afraid to die. I just don't want to be there when it happens,
– WOODY ALLEN

Wouldn't the last to-do
on anybody's list have to be
actually kicking the bucket?
Meanwhile, that's a dire term
for all the pleasures
we might still seek to enjoy
before we finally kick
(which is certainly the last
activity I have planned).

Doesn't that final bell-toll
belong in the total tally
of our not-to-be-missed events?
Face it: alongside birth,
it *is* the one certainty
right there at the end
like a bold, black full-stop,
whatever else we had planned.

Or maybe it doesn't belong
on such a list.
After all, to die isn't a thing
we ordinarily anticipate
with much enthusiasm,
even after advance directives
and wills are signed and sealed.

We may be insatiably
(or even morbidly) curious
about the fact of dying,
but we shrink from visualizing
it actually taking place,

even eventually, even
knowing it *is* in the so-called
order of things.

But then I have to recall
with love and nostalgia
one incomparable friend
who found herself impaled
on a shaft of pain so piercing
she longed for it all
to be over and done
rather than suffer a moment more
of unbearable, seemingly
endless laceration,
finally welcoming
her merciful reprieve.

I've had other lovely friends
who sometimes sank
into a pit so dark
they prayed to sleep past waking.

And speaking of prayer,
I offer my approving nod
to all you faithful spirits
trusting in your hearts
a Divine Consciousness
that offers free redemption
and eternal life in heaven
to every blessed one of us.

Or maybe you already know
you were born before
and will be again and again,
buckets be damned.

Not that fairy-godmother
aunt Mildred of mine,
as I never tire of telling.

Well into her old-maid eighties,
she lost all fear
of her impending end,
grew unconcerned
for what may lie beyond
in that undiscovered land
that sends us back
no useful news at all.

She assured me one night,
back in the sterile glare
of another emergency room,

Don't get me wrong, Donny.
I'm not afraid to die.
I'm afraid of what-all else
can still go wrong with me
before I finally do.

Though she sometimes
prayed not to wake,
I still have a lot to learn
about being that ready,
that fed up with it all.

Most would agree,
even in dire extremity,
we still have satisfactions
worth waking for:
a child's upcoming wedding,
one more festive holiday
among the bright wrappings,
the gleeful *wows* and *thank-you's*.
Even a healed incision
can be enough of an inducement
to keep you going if you're only
a few black-and-blue hours
home from a major surgery.

We may anticipate a new year
of Hollywood attractions,
or opportunities to further
some favorite cause,
maybe publication
of that book in head and heart
but not yet written or shared.

Sometimes a carefree sexcapade
can keep those pistons firing,
and *even*, if we dare,
might yet come another chance
at honest, ego-busting love.

Meanwhile, exotic spots
rank high on many a list.
How about the rare thrill
of standing swirled
in massive cascades
of synchronized fireflies
as we once did with friends
one warm twilit evening
up in the Smokies?

I also can't forget
an arching banyan tree,
heavy with the mass arrival
of countless scarlet macaws
screaming like maniacs
in the spattering patter
of a sudden Costa Rican rain.

I've even witnessed
with upturned, widened eyes
the marble *David,*
the cathedral at Cologne,
not to mention
the timeless grey towers
arrayed at Angkor Wat,

or, for that matter,
the Andromeda galaxy,
floating like a vast cocoon
above the trembling lenses
of my binoculars
as I stood dizzy
on a Georgia island beach.

I already suspect
that to list and seek
even more amazements
would be sheer greed.

And yet . . . the Parthenon,
still and weathered
atop my shrinking check-list.

I almost stood there too,
but opted to stay home
as friends flew off for Athens,
leaving me to groan
back here with prostate pain,
(which, believe you me,
was hardly an item
on my list at all).

So what's on yours?
Or maybe you haven't
pondered it all that often.
I've known folks who
couldn't recall such dreams.
They had buckets of luggage though
and sometimes an urge
to kick them all for good,
schlepping them along
wondering where or how
they might finally
lay their burdens down.

I, on the other hand,
still want to emulate
the lucky ones of you
who claim a *bona fide*
embarrassment
of fortune to savor and share,
ever willing to accept
humbly (and with pride as well)
our generous sampling of it all.

So if it's pyramids
on your personal list,
or a pot of beef stew
with crispy cornbread
like Mama used to cook,
or a flitting glimpse
of an almost-extinct bird
not reported on in years –
feel free to join me here
in this happy, lucky life
of hopeful optimism,
somehow sensing
(don't you?)
that you can't take it with you,
whatever it is
you're hanging on to –
or for.

2014

Losses

You'll lose some things along the way.
Some you won't even know are gone,
some you'll wonder about for years,
a few you'll sadly wish you still had
back in your grasp again.

My father's gold medal for debate
(Villa Rica, Georgia, 1915)
remained for years in my possession.
But countless folks, in and out
over the decades, included one
who stole from me.

Along my muddling way I've lost
the Boy Scout neckerchief slides I carved,
twenty-something merit badges too,
the knife with Scout emblem
I got for a winning slide in '59,
though I know where it is now:
rusting under the surf somewhere
just off the south end
of Sapelo Island, Georgia,
slipped from a hole in a pocket
(summer 1995).

My high school class ring,
though I know where it is too:
under the churning turbulence
at the foot of a waterfall
by the old covered bridge on Concord Creek
(Cobb County, Georgia, 1962)
where I splashed around with buddies
one summer afternoon.

I tossed a novel penciled in the Navy,
all about the life and girl I left behind.
She wore that ring on a chain
a quarter-century before I learned
how women could be my friends.
I've even lost the name of that book,
something like *The Way We Were.*

An ice-white quartz weapon,
heftier than an arrowhead
unearthed in the back yard
of a first-purchased home
(Lithia Springs, Georgia, 1972)
discarded with wrappings
after a second or third move.
Kids I helped to raise there,
grown and free now too.

Some of my hair, smooth skin,
good eyesight, hearing,
a bit of the spring in my step,
much innocence, some optimism –

finally to lose a corporal form,
dispersed right back eventually
amid the flinging stars
from whose great furnace hearts
all forms are forged –
this one once again included.

2012

Old & New

I leave Sisyphus at the foot of the mountain. The struggle itself toward the heights is enough to fill a man's heart. – ALBERT CAMUS

That youthful me
of nineteen-sixty-two
is old news now –
and this old me is new,
and less familiar too.

Indeed I'm also old,
the proverbially promised
seventy this year,
still pursuing, still maturing
with any luck, ripening
into a completion
I can't quite predict
or claim much credit for
before the least of me
dissipates away
into the dust and vapor
that was a conscious coil.

Born well back
in the turbulent midst
of the last century
(of the last millennium)
a fateful nineteen-forty-five
where ordinary objects
were fast morphing
from matter to energy,
credit to Dr. Einstein
and the bombs he so regretted,
I still have one fond foot
in the elder ways:
still scribble on lined paper,
still pad over to packed shelves
to find a favorite passage
for old time's sake.

Should my trove of sources
have sentiments
inside their dry-glue bindings,
they'd be wistful
that I come less often
to leaf through dog-eared
pages redolent of must,
looking for some old fact,
some timeless truth,
some detail I found meaningful
and underlined decades ago
with a sharpened gold
number-two pencil,
itself a curious artifact
like me these days.

I can easily Google it now,
though even this desktop
where a bright monitor
promptly pixels out
each perfect letter
I keyboard onto it
and pops up sources
with more minutiae
than I bargained for,
is fast becoming dated.

Why not a laptop,
a tablet, even an iPhone
with that bigger, better screen –
and why not speech
instead of keys to strike
with well-drilled fingers,
grateful as I am still
to dear Miss Lucille Hood
who taught us teens
on manual machines
what we then called
touch typing?

I'm morphing too:
cloudy cataracts no more,
clear silicone lenses,
reminding me
with bouquet vividness
how blue blue skies can be
how white great clumps of cloud,
how I now see my world
as sharp in crystal focus
as hairs on a fiddlehead.

Behind my ears bionic ears
that click and squeal
to send old/new sensations
of fluting birdsong,
song lyrics too,
no longer in that fog
of hampered hearing
(and not to mention
a mouth of crowns,
though none have yet
transmitted radio sounds
as some have done, they say,
or maybe will for me one day).

Why not even toss
this too, too solid
case of incarnation
we call a conscious brain,
render mortal flesh and bone
into far less perishable
circuits – dis-incarnate!
into a database,
a flash-drive chip,
a hi-res hologram
more present and real
than snowy Princess Leia,
stored in a cyber-cloud
aloft, aloof, careless

of humankind,
participant in a cosmos
that won't dissipate
whatever the earthly weather?

Might not such identity
give some ethereal *me*
at least the illusion
of freedom to roam
as I once did so happily
(with only occasional
disillusionments)
when I still shouldered
anew each welcome year
my rolling stone?

2016

Ageing

An aged man is but a paltry thing,
A tattered coat upon a stick, unless
Soul clap its hands and sing, and louder sing
For every tatter in its mortal dress. – WILLIAM BUTLER YEATS

Free at last, free at last . . . – MARTIN LUTHER KING

Subtle hints in recent years:
spot on a calf unhealed
as once it would have,
alien fog rolled in
on closing horn of ear,
squinting eye,
renegade belly
finally protesting
all it's stomached
over the carefree decades.

I wish someone
had told me, though,
how I'd celebrate
my seventies,
how I'd thank
that prescient grandfather
who traced my long lifeline
when I was maybe four.

A body just *will* age,
and wizen, and conclude,
even as a mind
may wise up somewhat,
until the soul, or spirit
(assuming such a thing,
and it's surely no mere thing)
may then be free.

2016

The Best Year of Your Life

Do you remember a few?
Can you choose just one?
The carefree year when bicycles ruled
and summer stretched endless?
A winter on a warm beach in Mexico?
Your wedding day and night
full of delights and omens?
(The day your divorce was final
with its relief and freedom?)

Or maybe you're one of those cheerful folk
claiming now is the all-time
time of your life, no matter what,
that *it's all good,* even the bad
for some sweet-lemon reason?

I can easily think that way,
living mostly free of troubles,
still indulging opportunities,
feeling a smidgin more aware, settled
after all my experiments with happiness,
with less left to prove these days.

But maybe in the scheme of things
my seventy-third year isn't that great.
Maybe I really would rather
be a third of those years again,
and would I want it to be this me,
knowing what I know now,
or ignorant and cocky as I was back then?

And either way,
how would that reliving be?

What would I say now, if I could,
to my 24-year-old self?

*You'll come to know
and be yourself, better.
You'll lose your taste
for thrills you never needed:
tobacco, false friends, fear, certainty.*

*Now's the time to prove yourself,
make your indelible mark –
but life is not a proving ground.*

*Look before you leap,
though all who hesitate are lost.*

*Pay no mind to this old man
dispensing oxymorons.*

My best friend and I
were high school seniors
when his mother cautioned us,
*Enjoy all this while you can
'cause these are your very best years.*

I guessed she spoke from experience
which made me apprehensive
about what might lie ahead
for us carefree kids,
though in my case at least,
she was mistaken.

I've had a lion's banquet
of best years since my salad days,
plus a few I might have skipped
though I probably shouldn't have,
even had it been possible.
It's good I weathered them,
took their unwelcome lessons.

I was in a group thing once
when a guy got up to brag

how much he valued his mistakes,
wrong turns, failed relationships,
drugs and other calamities –
since they'd all served him so well,
made him the man he was,
and on and on.

Our facilitator broke in with this:

*Look, if you have bad experiences,
you may as well learn something from them –
but is that your only way to learn?*

I came away thinking
how preferable the good times are,
enlightening too,
in ways nothing else can be,
hopefully even habit-forming,
how only a masochist would choose less,
how certain it is that worse
will come unbidden,
despite our best decisions and intentions.

We're lucky to get a few choice walk-on roles
and a life of our own beyond the scenes
in this long, engaging drama.

2019

Seventy-five

I've seen more yesterdays than I ever will tomorrows.
– JOE GRUSHECKY

You're in pretty good shape, for the shape that you're in. – DR. SEUSS

It is a milestone, no?
in the generous span we're lucky to get,
outliving by years our proverbial
promised three-score-and-ten.

Seventy-five years, though!
With considerable luck
and a modicum of discipline,
I'm still a work in progress.

2020

Apprehension

for Evie, going on five

Maintain a beginner's mind. – BUDDHIST MAXIM

Our ignorance
of fathomless mystery
prompts a grown-up urge
to comprehend
that undiscovered country,
to say we know, or even guess
what's really in it.

Let this enigma
recommend instead
the simple, innocent,
opposite unknowing
of a carefree four-year-old
unbothered by fear,
welcoming wonderment.

We smile from our comfortable
lawn chairs to watch her
scamper on grass-wet feet
across a twilit meadow
to snatch her first-
ever lightning bug
as it rises in wild rapport
with dozens of others,
each a little weaving beam
in the encroaching dark
we all have known
yet do not know.

She unfolds her fist
to discover what she has,
then watches wild-eyed
this minute, animated object

of her total attention
climb on black-wire legs
belly blinking, blinking
chartreuse-gold
up her upheld thumb,
then unsheathing in a flash
translucent wings
to weave away –
just like that!
a wandering star-spark,
a magic disappearing act –
or anything else
she might imagine.

2013

Gratitude

Let me ease into the luxury of gratitude
like kids in a bin of rainbow balls at McDonald's,
like a giddy bride in a thornless bed of roses
or a tipsy old man winging snow angels
while singing off-key carols on a winter lawn.

Let me be as confirmed and satisfied
as any cloistered monk, secured
in the empty plenitude of meditation –
even as Alice, tumbling down the rabbit hole,
heads to who knows what or when or where.

Surrender us willingly, every living one,
to fulfillment, grace, and gratitude,
since after all, we might not even be here,
and cannot fathom how we got to be –
and yet – quite haply – here we are.

20__

The End is Near!

In my end is my beginning. – T. S. ELIOT

Depending on the sort of end we're contemplating,
we may or may not be glad to see it arrive.
If it's the end of a famine on some far-flung continent,
it may be happy news we hadn't even heard of yet.

If it happened to be the end of my own life instead,
I might not know a lot about that either,
but should it come now, as Joan Rivers famously quipped,
not one of you will say with a sigh, *Oh, he died so young!*

For better or worse, things are forever ending.
Maybe it's the happy outcome of a difficult pregnancy
or the lamentable end of a trouble-free childhood
(not that I think any of us ever had one of those).

I recall the end of the instant I was rear-ended,
only to discover how decent and even apologetic
the driver of the other car turned out to be
(not to mention how well insured he was).

What about the end of an ordinary day, or
a marvelous one, or a days-long kidney stone attack?
What about the end of a night racked by weird dreams
like the curious one I just tossed myself through?

As I think about that escapade, the crucial part was
the tiger who chased my old pal and me up a treehouse
where we barricaded ourselves and threw bricks at him.
He then turned into a grinning simpleton, just poking fun.

The end of welfare as we knew it was a mixed blessing,
but so was the end of that interminable Vietnam War
when we consider how much less than nothing was gained,
the unspeakable losses to families who sacrificed sons.

But whether it's the end of a Hawaiian beach vacation
you and I wanted to last for a lifetime or more,
or the end of this damnable pestilence daunting us now,
it's just one more beginning, another tiger to tame.

2020

Last Words

Reported final utterances of the dying
are often not the words they really said.

(I've heard *Oh shit!* is the most common,
though hardly ever quoted after the fact.)

Surely some die silent,
peaceful even, well beyond
our wildest guessing.

These last words I know:

My mother's voice on the phone:
Just say a prayer
(and if I did, I can't remember now).

*I suppose this goes without saying,
but I do love you,*
I told him.

And I you, he echoed clearly
from his hard bed.

I turned and walked right out
of that fatal room for good.

My favorite one,
true or fabricated
(but easily believed, knowing him),
is credited to Oscar Wilde:

*This wallpaper and I
are fighting a duel to the death.
Either it goes or I do.*

2019

Resolution

gaiety transfiguring all that dread – WILLIAM BUTLER YEATS

Let me live and not go dying
angry, fearful, proud,
crying, blaming, still denying,
wanting more than lives allow.

May I use my time here singing,
laughing, loving, true –
ready then to leave it sighing
with a satisfied adieu.

Every story has an ending,
bitter, sweet, or sad.
May I meet my impending
resolution, and be glad.

2005

Epitaph

Oh the comfort, the inexpressible comfort of feeling safe with a person; having neither to weigh thoughts nor censor words, but pouring them all out – just as they are – chaff and grain together – certain that a faithful hand will take and sift them, keep what is worth keeping, and then, with the breath of kindness, blow the rest away.– WILLIAM ELLERY CHANNING

*And what the dead had no speech for, when living,
They can tell you, being dead: the communication
Of the dead is tongued with fire beyond the language of the living.
– T. S. ELIOT*

You'll speak to us whenever you are done.
Whatever bracing words you offered
when you were here in body, we'll remember.
They sound again now gently in mind's ear,
no matter when, in that same voice you had,
but stronger, clearer, truer now.

And all the useless, former follies
winnow out, like that chaff from grain.
The slips along your human path
by grace of Providence now dissipate
with all your scattered bones – so best truth,
best caring shine at last, now that you are done.

You'll love us yet, and better now –
timeless, unconditioned, flawless love
beyond the living love you had to give.
And we may hold that ripened fruit at last,
ruddy, fallen from the tree of life
into our upturned open hands.

Embraces once shared will hold us now
as they happily did those years before.
And salty tears will wash our eyes to see:
the best of you is now this part of us.
We know that you are here and with us,
now that all the rest is done.

199_

Promethean

A moth in fragile flight
pursues a point of light,
blinded to temerity,
flits with fine celerity
from dewy dark of night.

Homing near and near,
its body cracked and sere,
it ends upon a perfect pyre,
purified by fatal fire.
So much at last is clear.

1972

Not to Change the Subject, but . . .

It's the end of the world as we know it – and I feel fine. – R. E. M.

The viral death toll mounts without relent,
but a neighbor brought us a plump, near-ripe tomato,
seed from Greece, he said.

Half the nation now is convinced the other half is crazy,
but our stroll down by a woodland creek we just discovered
was easy, arm-in-arm, joking, jostling each other like teenagers.

More hurricanes have ravaged the Gulf Coast,
but a Pensacola friend called to say she's fine
and has now re-read all the Harry Potter books.

Cities and forests are still aflame,
but today we're calm and overcast here,
a bit cool for early September.

If we take the long view, we're all tragic, terminal histories,
but that tomato was undeniably flavorful,
and my back'll get scratched again tonight, just where it itches.

2020

Andy's Ride on the Merry-go-round

Take this waltz. – LEONARD COHEN

Don't you cry, Andy; now don't make a sound.
See, this is your ride on the merry-go-round!

Your father's looking, and he paid your fare.
He wants you to love it. He's right there.

So don't cry, Andy, and don't feel bad.
Ride to the music. Wave to your dad.

As it spins and whirls you round,
hold the pole. Don't look down.

Don't be afraid of anything.
Hear the happy rhythm ring.

It's a waltz tune. Don't let go.
Soon you'll be spinning slow,

and in good time, your ride is done.
Then you'll think it was so much fun.

Then you'll wish you could ride again
and fret because you've reached the end.

But don't cry, Andy. No, don't even frown.
We each get one ride on this merry-go-round.

1972

Acknowledgements

Countless supportive, encouraging people over many years and more recently have made this my first published book possible.

I credit most that favorite aunt of mine, noted throughout the book, a veteran fourth-grade teacher who first made me want to teach – and to make poems. She loved to recite them and sing songs, including many that I never forgot.

One day long ago Mrs. Katharine Hood burst into our fifth-grade classroom and sashayed around our desks singing naNAH, naNAH, naNAH, naNAH. Finally she turned and announced, "Poetry has *rhythm!*" She not only fostered my love for poems and songs she taught us; she demonstrated how much fun teaching could be.

Bob Coyle! He taught me high school English, sponsored the school paper I co-edited, inspired me to follow in his footsteps, headed the English department where I first taught, and remained my oldest best friend for the rest of his long life. He was so candid about poems of mine he didn't like that I could trust his approval of the ones he did. His wife Gay has also read much of my work and encouraged my efforts.

I owe a lot to my former wife, Barbara Littig, who inspired some of these poems. Besides making a home and raising two outstanding boys with me, she often listened to poems I was writing and revising and reciting to her throughout the seventies. She also had copies of many of them printed for me to share.

Franklin Abbott (whose generous comments are on the back cover) has invited me often to read poems at events around Atlanta, went with me to visit BookLogix where I was finally published, and, without flattery, has consistently urged me to trust my efforts, share them – and not do it hoping for a prize.

Rob Stuart, a best friend, fellow traveler, and confidant for years, has appreciated and critiqued much of my work. He's a Presbyterian minister and a poet in his own right whose Christmas cards have always included a new poem to mark the season. His insights about my poems have been invaluable.

Helen Hardin, also a best friend and correspondent, has read and studied countless poems with me, including my own, for years, long since she was a student in my English classes. She has carefully, thoughtfully read my manuscript and critiqued it kindly and candidly. I expect she'll be as happy as anyone to see this project done at last.

Jessica Parker at BookLogix sat down with me for an hour last year and got me right on track putting this book together. Since that visit with her, I became more convinced than ever that I could get it all completed, which I have done with her ongoing support and expertise.

Tom West, a best friend and confidant for decades, is a professional graphic designer in Atlanta who has completed the formatting and artwork here, in particular the cover he designed. He's solved many technical problems that had me stumped and has made valuable suggestions along the way.

Marti Olesen, an astute friend I taught with for several years and have exchanged poems with from time to time, has critiqued my work and helped me with decisions about what to include or leave out. She's another one who doesn't mince words, which is just what any aspiring writer needs.

Margaret Schaeffer was a neighbor and friend of my aunt's in Cedar Key who wrote poetry and attended a writer's workshop I led at the Island Hotel back in the '80's. After reading some of these poems, she thought I had "bared my soul," which no doubt I have, but she believed my poems deserved a wider audience. I wish I could give her a copy of *Hearts* now since she was one of the first ones who urged me to publish.

Sharyn Kane and Richard Keeton are a married couple and accomplished free-lance writers who taught in Fulton County's Arts in the Schools program when I was teaching gifted education at Milton High School. I invited them to visit my classes often and sat with my students practicing skills they taught us. Not only did they give me creative ideas for my own teaching, but they instilled a deep respect for their profession, expressed confidence in my writing ability, and encouraged me to do more with it. I doubt they realize what a powerful example they set and how it helped get me to this point in my own work.

Mike Riley and I graduated Douglas County High together in 1963 but then went our separate ways. He's now a retired college professor with expertise in book-binding and children's literature. He's also written a fine detective series that I've read with pleasure and look forward to seeing published. Since our recent reconnecting, he's read my manuscript carefully and offered many suggestions that have made it better.

Last and most of all, Gilson de Assis Satel: As partner and now husband, he has made the past thirteen years of my life a rare adventure I never thought I'd have. He's listened to so many of my poems, offered insights, and helped me choose my title and cover photo. Anyone who reads *Hearts Bigger than Brazil* will see that it would never have happened without him.

Other relatives and friends have indulged me by reading or listening to me read my poems over the years, offered good suggestions and encouragement, and helped me get it all done. I'm in your debt and I thank you all.

Note: Earlier drafts of a few poems have appeared elsewhere: "Star of Venus" in *Cold Mountain Review*; "Old Rhythms" in *Calamaro*; "Was Melville Also Gay" in the anthology, *This Assignment is So Gay*; and several poems in *RFD* magazine.